Some Through
the Waters

Some Through the Waters

by
Clare Bauer

Thomas Nelson Publishers
Nashville • New York

ISBN 0-8407-5687-9

To Conn,
whose constant love and gentle strength
gave me a glimpse of God long before I met Him.

Acknowledgments

Nobody writes a book alone, I'm sure, but in my case there are a lot more than a few to whom I will always be grateful. To Jeni Strouss, whose encouragement to write came years before I knew I wanted to; to Brenda Arnold, whose careful editing and loving comments made the script readable; to Joyce Landorf, who not only prayed for me and wrote to me and called me, but who also gave me the title and the determination to finish the book when it would have been so much easier to quit; and finally and most of all, to my dear family: Conn, Julie and Carl, Beck and Larry, Lisa and David, Nancy, and Jon— for their help, their humor, and their rich, rich love!

Contents

Foreword

All of us at one time or another see depicted on the evening TV news a story of a fire or flood disaster. Idly we wonder what our lives and responses would be if it were happening to our house or to our loved ones.

However, tucked away in our minds is the thought that God simply would never let *that* happen to us. It is as if tragedies will happen to others but certainly not to me and my house.

The truth is that these things—"these firey trials," as Peter said—can and do happen to the children of God.

This book is Clare Bauer's candid response to a major disaster which involved her and the lives of her family.

Our disasters, crises, and tragedies may differ from Clare's, but her articulate response is one that I want to remain with us to be recalled when we may need it.

Of the whole experience, Clare's own words are eloquent and revealing when she writes, "The one thing we can count on is that we are not alone and God will supply whatever we need.

"There is sometimes a time lag between our knowing that and our experiencing it, and occasionally we are put in what seems to be an endless holding pattern; but God will never fail us. He cannot!"

This book then is for all of us who, from time to time, go through the waters of heartache, suffering, or disaster.

This book says: Look up! God is in this. God will never fail us. He cannot!

Joyce Landorf

In shady green pastures, so rich and so sweet,
God leads His dear children along;
Where the water's cool flow bathes the weary one's feet,
God leads His dear children along.
Some thro' the waters, some thro' the flood,
Some thro' the fire, but all thro' the blood;
Some thro' great sorrow, but God gives a song;
In the night season and all the day long.

—*"God Leads Us Along" by G.A. Young*

1

Home, Home on the Range

It stands there, massive and brooding and lonely, its logs aged to silver from the buffeting of the harsh winds of winter and the rains of spring and fall, dappled by the shadows of a thousand leaves in the sunlight of summer. It is older now than many of the people who live in the valley, but all of them, young and old, know it simply as the Old Log House. Some forgotten ancestor with tremendous foresight had planned to set the house far back from the dusty road that leads to the little town of St. Anthony. For more than half a century the house has stood there, nestled in the same grove of sycamore and cottonwood trees that protected its predecessor, a small frame house the family built when they first purchased the farm in 1908. Grandfather Bauer had paid $37.50 an acre for the farm. The small house has long since disappeared; for years only a slight depression in the lawn remained to indicate it had ever existed. Massive stone pillars guarded the pathways that led to the front and back doors of the house.

My husband, Conn, had grown up in this Idaho farmhouse, and the heritage of both farmer and pioneer that is such a part of this section of the country gave him a tremendous love for everything about the place. The two hundred acres of rich ground that surround the house are irrigated from the Teton River, which flows along the south edge of the farm. With our two youngest children,

Nancy, then thirteen, and Jonathan, nine, we had moved there in 1974. It offered a very different way of life from the hectic pace we had experienced in California, where we had lived for more than twenty years. Conn had been a building contractor in the San Francisco Bay area of northern California. There we had raised our family of five children—four daughters and a son. By 1974, the older girls were married. Julie lived with her husband, Carl, in southern California; Lisa and David were in San Jose; and Becky and Larry lived in Texas.

Conn's love of the land should have been a part of my nature, too. My maternal grandfather had homesteaded land in that same area with such fervor that he had become known as a land baron. But all my instincts told me city life had a lot of advantages, and I loved the fast pace of our urban life-style. We had visited the farm many times over the years, and it was always with a sense of relief that I started the trip back to California. "Idaho is a great place to visit, but I would really hate to live there!" I would say as we drove away from the farm after another dreary vacation, and because Conn didn't verbally disagree I jumped to the conclusion that he agreed. Years later I realized he had never responded with any answer at all. It turned out that he felt precisely the opposite!

He came home from his office one day in early 1974, and as we sat in the study talking over the day he casually said, "I have been thinking, honey. Pete wants to buy out the business and I think I would like to sell it to him and retire early."

"Great!" I responded, thinking that an early retirement for a man of forty-six would probably be in four or five years. By then, Jon and Nancy would be old enough that we could finally do the traveling we had always wanted to do. I get a lot of exercise jumping to conclusions. It turned out he had not yet finished his sentence.

12

"What I had in mind was selling the place here and all four of us moving in June to Idaho, and living there on the farm!"

I couldn't believe what my ears were hearing! He was not famous for his practical jokes, but I desperately hoped he was trying out one of his worst. I looked at him to see if there was a clue on his face, and realized to my horror that he was dead serious. "What do you think of that?" he said, misreading my shock for pleasure.

I didn't think I should tell him what I was thinking, but privately I decided that maybe this was a sort of male menopause, or perhaps a touch of temporary insanity that would pass soon without too many complications. I think I muttered something profound like "Yippee," and said I thought it was time for dinner.

For the next few months we talked a lot about his decision. First I tried sweet reasoning with him. I pointed out how comfortable we were in California, how nice it was to be close to the girls and their husbands and all our friends, how great the schools were, how nice it was to be near San Francisco for shopping and the ballet and the theater, what a great church we were involved in, and how nice it was not to have to shovel snow off the driveway in January.

He pointed out, just as reasonably, how clean the air was on the farm, how quiet it was up there away from all the traffic sounds, how great the fishing and winter sports were going to be, and how nice it would be not to have to mow the lawn in February!

I tried crying. That had less effect than reasoning, and I looked as if I had a perpetual cold. Unlike many movie stars, I do not look pretty when I cry.

Now if tears hadn't worked, and speaking softly had failed, I decided I had better do something desperate, so I started to pray. I told God that Conn was simply not listening and was about to make the most terrible mistake of our marriage. So I asked God to speak to Conn and make His will very clear to him. Then, at peace with myself at last, I told God that whatever He wanted to do was fine with me.

It turned out that what He wanted was for Conn to lead the family. As time went on, it became very clear that we were definitely going to be at home on the range— Idaho's range, that is.

We sold the big home we had built so lovingly eight years earlier in Monte Sereno, with the prayer that the family who would live there would not only love it as we had loved it, but would also find Christ there, as we had. With mixed emotions of sadness and anticipation for our new life-style, we watched the two moving vans being filled with the accumulations of twenty-five years of married life. On the morning of June 15, we followed the vans down the driveway, away from the house and friends I felt certain we would never find the likes of again. But I was discovering, as I yielded my will to God's, a real sense of peace that this move was not a mistake after all, but really exactly what God wanted for all of us.

The drive to Idaho lasted two very long, hot days. The heat and weariness of the trip was gently soothed by the coolness and quiet of the big old farmhouse. After we were settled to a certain degree, we began to get reacquainted with the area.

Located in the southeastern corner of the state, we are bounded by the Rocky Mountains on the east and the north. The main industry in Idaho is agriculture, and the large rivers and streams that abound over the state are literally its lifeblood. The land had been wrested from the desert years before by stubborn pioneers who saw a vision of virgin soil that would produce bountiful crops if there were only enough water. They had captured the rivers in a system of dams and reservoirs throughout the state, and it had become what they had envisioned.

But farm prices fluctuate, and as they drifted steadily downward through the years, the area had increasingly shown the effects of a depressed economy. It is called by the people here, "Next Year Country." When one asks why, the answer comes easily, "If things don't work out this year, there is always next year." It sounds hopeful at first, but everyone knows there is no guarantee for next year either. Rather than being hopeful, it becomes a dirge of despair.

We were only there a short time when we discovered that the greatest item of local interest was the Teton Dam. It had been under construction for several years and was now only a couple of years from completion. Located in a steep, wooded canyon about ten miles due east of the farm, it was a welcome project in the area. The workers stimulated the local economy by their need for housing and other services. In general, the project had given a real boost to the sagging spirits of the community. The federal government, which was in charge of building the dam, had not forgotten this tiny corner of the world after all!

While most of the people in the area welcomed the building of the dam, some were bitterly opposed to the project when it was first proposed in 1968. Environmentalists believed it would do untold and irreparable damage to the flora and fauna of the area.

Then there were those who said it should not be built in that particular location because it could never survive the pressures of the water due to the nature of the canyon's shale rock. They battled the project without letup, and ultimately without success, as they took their battle from one court to another in a vain attempt to keep the monster from dwelling in the canyon. Their dire predictions of doom were greeted with either patronage or hostility.

The purpose of the dam was threefold. It was to provide flood control, recreation, and irrigation water storage. Every spring, as the winter snows began to melt in the mountains, the Teton went on her annual rampage. Early in June, when the runoff waters were high, the river would routinely overrun her banks, causing a commotion for a few days. Area farmers and volunteers from the nearby towns of St. Anthony and Teton City would be called out to stand up to their waists in the freezing water, sandbagging the river banks. This overflow was so predictable that it became an annual "nonevent," and was considered more of a nuisance than a real danger.

Once every few years, when the ice was very thick and the winter had been unusually severe, the Teton's flooding would create several days of inconvenience, with water in basements and on highways, disrupting traffic. But it really couldn't be classified as a major catastrophe by anyone, except perhaps the irate housewife who had to clean up the mucky mess!

The construction of the dam was fascinating to both Conn and Jon, but after a couple of visits to the site I quickly lost interest. The men in hard hats, the huge yellow trucks, the earth-moving equipment, and the derricks were so far below our viewpoint high in the canyon that the whole thing seemed quite unreal to me. I thought about how very quickly we would be able to drive there if we wanted to water ski or picnic or fish. But beyond that, the dam had no place whatsoever in my thoughts.

The fact that it was directly east of the farm and less than twenty minutes away by car was never really very significant to me. The question of what would happen to us if it should ever fail never crossed my mind. I had read for years with great interest accounts of disasters such as the Johnstown flood in Pennsylvania. One of the things I found fascinating was the reaction of the people involved. I suppose it is totally human never to expect you will be a statistic! Besides, I did not consider the dam a threat because I knew no federal dam had ever failed.

We worked hard those first two years to restore the house and the farm to what we believed it could and should be. After years of renters and transient living, the house was in a shabby state, and there was so much of it! With its three stories and full basement, revamping the structure was an overwhelming task even to think about.

Fifty years of accumulated multilayered wallpaper (painted over and then repapered) defied all the steamers, razor blades, putty knives, and elbow grease we could put into it. Underneath all the layers were lovely smooth plaster walls, but a thousand times over I had despaired of ever finding them.

The floors of the old house were solid oak, nearly two inches thick, and their warm golden tones gleamed through in spite of all the grime and traffic of a thousand feet pounding across them through the years.

The windows were warped and stiff, and some of them had been painted shut. I vented my displeasure at the sloppy painters as we worked at loosening the windows. When we finally got them open, we discovered that all the screens were missing or needed replacing. And there were mosquitos by the millions just outside the windows, waiting for a free lunch from anyone dumb enough to go to the trouble of opening the wretched windows.

The kitchen was the sort of homemaker's nightmare that no one would deliberately plan. Like Topsy, it had apparently just "growed" over the years, and by the time we moved in it had almost become a joke. The old-fashioned cooking range was in one corner; you worked at it with your back to the only light, a dim bulb in the center of the high ceiling. The cast iron sink, now chipped and corroded, was in another corner and its leaking pipes were covered by a modest and tattered skirt. A dilapidated table sat in the third corner. In the fourth was a high, narrow cabinet that had apparently tried to serve as a china closet, pantry, and working counter, and from the looks of it had succeeded at none of them. The refrigerator, considered a vital part of my kitchen for years, stood forlornly in another room. The sixteen-foot square room was large enough to become a kitchen but how it failed to do so through the years was beyond my imagination.

Through a door in the kitchen was a room called the sunporch. I never exactly knew why it was called that, except that it was a sort of porch, glassed in on all three sides by tiny paned windows, and it did definitely trap the sun. When the summer sun streamed in, the heat became unbearable in a hurry, because all but two of the windows were stationary. The only two that could be opened were on the west end of the porch. They opened from the top, with a hinge at the bottom, and so, when the unwary moved the latch, they were very apt to receive a smart rap on the head. To my great frustration, I discovered that even after you acquired the dexterity necessary to open the windows on the sunporch, it usually was far too hot to enjoy being there except in the very early morning. It was too hot in the summer, that is. In the winter, which can be seven or eight months long in Idaho, the sunporch was much too cold to use because it was not heated in any way.

Above the porch was a balcony. Although it added to the rather picturesque beauty of the house, the balcony was also unusable. Its floor, which formed the ceiling of the porch, was of tarpaper. In the summer, the black paper oozed tar and grew blisteringly hot. Anyone who tried to sunbathe on the balcony quickly learned two never-to-be-forgotten lessons. They understood, first of

18

all, how it felt to walk through fire, and second, they had black-stained feet for the rest of the summer.

Having neither the time nor the inclination to do much sunbathing, I could have lived with the tarpaper roof. Its biggest drawback, in my opinion, was that when the balcony caught and held the snow it leaked like a sieve. Anything that happened to be stored on the sunporch below (and storage seemed its only useful function) would get soaked if it were not moved away from the leaks. After the second winter I began to suspect the leaks were moving, because no matter where I moved something, it would soon be soggy.

The porch was a source of great irritation to me, and several times I suggested to Conn that we remove it. But whenever I suggested it to him (and admittedly, it may not have been *what* I said but *how* I said it), it seemed almost as if I thought we should burn Grandfather Bauer in effigy. Conn did not receive the suggestion well. It seemed that everything about the old house, including that irritating porch, had some great childhood memory for Conn, and he could never bring himself to change anything. I came at last to the very sage conclusion that the worst mistake a woman could make is to move into her husband's childhood home!

During the first two years in the house, in spite of the porch and a thousand other sacred cows, we gradually scraped and polished and sanded through all the layers and found we had a real gem on our hands. The old walls were nearly fourteen inches thick, and the pink sandstone of the fireplace that covered one wall of the living room became a lovely focal point for the room after we finally sandblasted all the layers of paint from it. Because it had been built in a time when fireplaces were used for heating as well as for appearance, we found that a fire in the fireplace warmed not just our hearts, but the whole first floor of the house as well.

We completely remodeled the kitchen. I had come to the conclusion in my first thirty minutes there that either the old kitchen went or I would, and to Conn's credit he only had to think a few minutes before he chose me. We knocked out a wall between the old kitchen and a back porch, added a pantry, new appliances, a bright yellow floor, and wallpapered the ceiling so that it danced with brilliant flowers. From the windows I could see the lovely lawns that surround the house, with the beds of flowers and bulbs I had planted the first year. Gradually I relaxed, realizing we were really home again.

Conn was more content than I had ever seen him. I'm sure he thoroughly enjoyed his work in California, especially in the early years while it was still a great challenge to him. But now I knew that his heart had always been here, and he felt fulfilled as a man in a way I had never seen before. He loved the farm and the work involved. It was his heritage, and he was thoroughly at home, working the land with the man we had hired to manage it for us while we were still living in California.

Conn taught Jon to work the land and to love it in the process, as his father had once taught him. And I watched with real joy as I saw the love bond growing between Conn and Jon. Together they repaired the old barn and painted the machine shed, and as they worked Conn shared his boyhood memories with Jon. Jon, without being aware of it, was in the process of making memories of his own.

Nancy had a difficult time adjusting to the life-style we now shared. She was a California child, and everything in her life had been oriented to the suburbs. Now, suddenly, it was life on the farm, and she didn't like it one little bit. Instead of her pretty pink bedroom overlooking the swimming pool, with friends calling on the telephone to talk for hours, she was faced with a bedroom where the wallpaper was peeling and the only swimming avail-

able was in the local river! She had always been re-
served, and as much as she needed friends she still found
it very difficult to reach out to strangers. There was even,
horror of horrors, a large garden. Nancy had always
assumed vegetables grew in the supermarket. Now she
found that along with the vegetables grew weeds, and
someone had to pull the weeds in the hot summer sun.
That somebody turned out to be her.

Autumn came just in time to save her from the stoop
labor, and life began to improve as she started high
school. She had always been a very good student, and
although it was hard for her to become accustomed to the
different ways of doing things in Idaho, she soon began to
make new friends and begin a new way of life. To her
utter delight, Nancy learned that Idaho allows its citizens
to drive an automobile at the tender age of fourteen. Her
greatest moment came when, on her fifteenth Christmas,
she found the keys to a used Karmann Ghia sports car
under the tree. She drove the car everywhere, and it
quickly became one of her favorite possessions.

Jon was in fourth grade when he started school that
first fall in Idaho. In a lot of ways his education was just
beginning. He learned very quickly that as the new kid in
school he had to work his way up the pecking order.
When he came home bloody and bruised the third day in
a row, I was more than a little upset. He calmed me down
by saying quietly, "Don't worry, Mom. I just have to
beat up three more guys, and I won't have to fight quite
so much after that!" Only three? I thought, "Thank
goodness, it's a small school!"

We had only been in Idaho a short time when our
oldest daughter, Julie, and her husband, Carl, decided to
move there, too. When they came through Idaho the
previous summer on their vacation, they fell in love with
the quiet countryside, and together with their three-
month-old daughter, Rebecca, they came. After a few

months, Carl found work and a home for them in the nearby town of Rexburg. It was so much fun for all of us to be close again after living such a long distance from each other.

Life fell into a rather predictable pattern after a time. It was interesting to be back in a climate with definite seasons after so many years in the perpetual summer of California. As fall came we found we were looking forward to the long winter with its skiing and other winter sports, and evenings by the fire in the living room. When the first snow fell we were all enchanted by its beauty. We laughed at the first blizzard and reveled in the wild wind and slashing snow. We all learned to ski together, and found that some of the best ski resorts in the country were within an hour's drive of the farm.

We took long walks through the frozen quiet and listened as our boots squeaked in the snow. The land was wintry and hushed around us, and we often walked in the blackness of the early winter nights, with millions of stars blazing so clearly, so close that it seemed you could reach out and touch them. We would return to the house with freezing noses, fingers, and toes, but a feeling of well-being made the world seem a very safe and pleasant place. The inconvenience of being snowed in or of sliding off the road into a snowdrift were offset by the fact that there was always a friendly neighbor willing to help dig out.

Spring came again, predictably, according to the calendar. It did not turn out to be one of those storybook climate changes that come gently and with some class. It was muddy and cold and long in coming. But after awhile, on the south side of the house at the base of the sunporch, some brave crocuses poked their heads through the snow, and I decided spring was going to come after all. As the snow melted and the flowers and bulbs started to bloom, I thought I had never seen colors so vivid. To this day I don't know if they are really brighter here or if they just seem that way after the long months of winter whiteness!

The seasons came and went, and as our third Idaho summer approached, we began planning for it as if we had lived there all our lives. Only one thing would definitely be different, we could be sure, in that spring of 1976. As our nation prepared to celebrate its two hundredth birthday, we would not have to fight the annual battle of the overflowing Teton. The new dam, scheduled for completion in the fall and already beginning to fill, would forever take care of that problem.

2

Beginnings

I was born in the southeastern part of Idaho in the fall of 1931. The sun on that lovely Indian summer day was warm, my mother recalled. We lived in a white frame house that overlooked the canyon of the wide, twisting river called the Snake. It winds its way from the mountains that are its birthplace and makes the valley bloom from early spring until the crops are harvested in the fall. The fields spread across the vast flood plain and begin their gentle ascent to the rolling foothills; from there, the land rises sharply to the rugged mountains that ring the valley—the Sawtooth range to the west and the Grand Tetons to the east.

My parents were working as farmers for my maternal grandparents at the time. Granddad Harrigfeld was one of the largest land owners in the valley. He had come to America from Germany in 1890 and settled first in Nebraska with his family. On hearing of the vast land in the West, open to those who were willing to homestead the wilderness, he came to Idaho to see for himself if the stories he had heard of the land's fertility and vastness were true. On seeing the endless sweep of open range covered with vegetation, he wept with joy. He *knew* he had found what he had sought all his life, a place to build a new life for himself and his growing family. He commissioned a man to build a home for the family and returned to Nebraska to bring them to Idaho.

"It's a new world out there!" he told his wife and children with great excitement. "It will be hard work to clear the land and build a farm, but it will be worth all it costs us. Land is the only investment you cannot lose. Hold onto it forever. Never sell it or let it go."

The family had to pay a much greater price than they had dreamed. When they reached their destination, my grandmother wept as my grandfather had, but for a different reason. There was no house; it had not even been started. And so the family spent the first long, incredibly cold winter in a sod house, frightfully inadequate for their needs. Their infant son, August, who was born that fall, died during the winter. His tiny body was buried in the windswept little cemetery a mile from the house.

Spring finally came, and with it the promise of production from the land. But the work was almost unbearably hard, and everyone over school age was expected to work as long and hard as any of the men. Through it all, Grandfather Harrigfeld knew the land was worth the price, and instilled in each of his children the same love and enthusiasm that was his. "Work hard for the land, and someday it will be your heritage," was his constant, if unspoken, covenant with his children.

My dad's parents lived not far from the Harrigfelds, but his family had a far different feeling for the land. "It was one way to make a living, and you could do it if all else failed," seemed to be the family motto in their house! Dad hated farming from the time he could pronounce the word, and as soon as he could he escaped from it and went to work in the copper mines of Utah. That was where my parents began their married life, and they lived there until the Depression of the 1930s drove them back to Idaho.

Being forced to work as a farmer for his father-in-law did not change my dad's mind about farming one whit. It only made him more inventive about ways of escape, and

26

more and more, as time wore on, he escaped from the daily grind by hunting and fishing in the woods and streams that came to the very edge of the farm. His apparent lack of concern and ambition irritated and angered both my mother and my grandfather. They could not understand his lack of interest in the farm, and he, for his part, felt they took the whole business far too seriously! Inevitably a confrontation came. Dad and Mom left the farm and moved into the small town of Ashton a few miles away. There Dad started a farm equipment business.

I was blissfully unaware of my parents' multitude of problems in those early childhood years. They were times of long winters when Dad often hitched up the team of horses to a creaking open sled and, bundled so tightly that only our eyes were visible, we rode across the frozen fields to a neighbor's house for supper and the card games that went on far into the night. We usually fell asleep on the host's bed after playing hide-and-seek in the delicious darkness of the bedrooms and the chilly attic. I never remember going home from those evenings; I was always sound asleep.

Our closest neighbor and my only friend, a little boy my age named Billy Garz, lived down the road, half a mile from our house. I often trudged through the summer dust that covered the road to play with Billy, picking wild flowers as I went along. He fascinated me, partly because he was the same size I was and partly because Billy, unlike me, was allowed to have candy whenever he wanted.

Dad started his farm equipment business in Ashton, and for the next fifteen years we lived in a two-story house on a large corner lot. Dad soon found out he was not cut out for business any more than he had been for farming, as he much preferred to spend time at the business next door to his—the town pool hall. No business can long endure an absentee owner, and Dad's was no exception. Gradually, in order to have money for operating capital, he and Mom began selling her farm land. Torn between wanting to help Dad and her impassioned belief in the security of land, arguments over money became more and more bitter, and our home became more of a battleground than a haven. Because it happened over a period of time, however, I thought all marriages were like my parents' and all homes were like ours. It made me shudder to think I would have to face that some day. It never occurred to me not to marry; after all, everyone did!

I had every intention of studying nursing after I finished high school until, in my senior year, I met Conn Bauer. We were at a high school youth group picnic on Sunday afternoon, when I looked over and saw for the first time the tall, blond young man who was to become my husband. He seemed so aloof from the rest of the crowd that I thought for a minute he must be somebody's older brother acting as chaperone. I don't even remember how we started talking, but I do remember I was completely and forever impressed. Nearly six feet, seven inches tall, Conn towered over the rest of the group, and his quiet strength made the other young men look awfully immature. I realized somewhere in our conversation that he didn't do much talking, but he must have said something right; we had arranged our first date before the afternoon was half gone!

When we got home from the date that night, I told my mother I had met the man I was going to marry.

That turned out to be an extremely accurate prophecy. Before long we were thinking and talking about marriage as if it were a foregone conclusion. Twice in the next few months I tried to break the engagement. As I watched my parents' marriage going from bad to worse, I decided maybe marriage wasn't such a good idea. Each time

Conn gently insisted that marriage did not have to be that way at all.

In the end I believed him. Shortly after my seventeenth birthday we were married. It was a beautiful formal wedding in the little community church, with the late autumn sun streaming through the stained glass windows. The only hitch came when Dad, who was to give me away, was late. True to form, he had gone duck hunting and forgotten the time! But Dad was, as usual, totally charming and completely bewildered that anyone would think he could possibly miss such an important occasion. As we started down the aisle he told me the hunting had been great. (I spent the rest of the walk wondering if he meant his hunt for ducks or mine for a husband!) And so a few minutes after four in the afternoon, I became Conn's bride. I wanted desperately to believe that Conn was right, that our marriage would be different and precious and alive, nothing like the marriages I already knew about.

Our honeymoon was a short one, not because Conn wanted it that way but because I couldn't wait to get home and begin to be a wife. The farm harvest had been a poor one that year, and both Conn and I took jobs in town to make ends meet. We were so poor that a mouse who had the great misfortune to choose our house as a dwelling place for himself and his family starved to death when he fell into our empty sugar bin! I looked at the poor thing with both pity and revulsion, wondering if his dying there was a sign of anything.

Our first Christmas was very special because it was ours. On Christmas Eve we drove out into the foothills near our house and Conn cut a small, fat, blue spruce tree covered with fragrant berries. We brought it home and decorated it with a lonely string of lights. We decided it was definitely the prettiest tree either of us had ever seen. Then, in place of the gifts we didn't have under the tree, we asked each other what we would like to have and to give if we were wealthy without limit. When Conn asked me what I would like more than anything, I told him of three things that would be the greatest gifts I could ever receive.

The first was a marriage that would increase and blossom with love so tender and precious that it would not only withstand any difficulty or hardship that came its way but also be more beautiful and vital because of that hardship. I told him I wanted to be more in love with him in twenty-five years than I was that night, and even as I said the words I knew it must be impossible.

The second thing I wanted was children who would not just enjoy each other in their childhood as very special friends, but who would someday, as adults, be even closer—even though miles and circumstances and successes or failures might separate them.

And finally, last but most important (and to me the most impossible of all) I wanted a security, a covering that could never fail me. I wanted something I could put my deepest hopes and dreams and confidences in and know that it would not collapse in the very moment I needed it the most. In that long-ago Christmas of 1948, I knew of nothing that could possibly promise me the security I needed with all my heart. But after all, we were only wishing!

Years later I was to find the answer to all those needs in a friend named Jesus. But on that special Christmas Eve more than thirty years ago, I never dreamed He would give me not only all I asked for but also a thousand other things besides.

Winter came and went that year, and in the spring a new crop went into the ground. By fall, we knew that the same cycle of poor crops and low prices had been repeated, and again we both took outside jobs to pay the bills. That continued for three years, except that after the first two Conn had to work alone, as our first daughter, Julie, had been born. Within eighteen months she was followed by a sister, Beck, and as the harvest came and went again we were forced to see that farming was a great way to live if you could afford it, but it was rapidly becoming apparent that it was a luxury we could no longer afford. So in the fall of 1953, we packed up all we had in a small trailer and moved to California, where we heard there was plenty of work and high wages. It was in some ways a difficult move, but because we believed it was the only option open to us, it was exciting, too. People are not afraid of change if it is their idea; it is only when they lose control and are forced into a new circumstance that they panic. This one we knew we could handle—after all, we were young and strong and in love.

And for a while, we did. We moved to southern California, which was experiencing a building boom, and Conn found work immediately. Because he was strong and ambitious and willing to work harder than anyone else on the job, he moved up in a hurry. Before long he was the foreman on three different jobs. I don't know how many more he would have tackled had he not been stricken suddenly with spinal paralytic polio.

In the five days before an accurate diagnosis was made, his weight slipped from 230 pounds to 175, and he was one very frightened young man. When he was admitted at last to the hospital, he was so weak he could barely move, and because he had never been ill in his life he was also very angry. How could God do something like this to him when he had only tried his best to do what was right for himself and his family?

While I was fighting the battle of fear and depression at home (how would I support our family, which now consisted of Lisa as well as Julie and Beck?), Conn was in the hospital struggling both to breathe and to bargain with God. *Get me out of this thing,* he promised silently, *and I will be your man as long as I live!* And then, in the middle of the long, long night, he felt a deep sense of peace that everything would indeed be all right. Not that he would necessarily be whole and healthy, as he wanted, but that somehow, even if he wasn't, God would tenderly care for him and for the rest of us. A long time later, he told me it was as if he were a small, hurting child climbing into his father's strong arms and knowing the comfort and security that only a father's loving strength can give. Ten days later he walked out of the hospital, his left arm useless and held in a brace to protect the shoulder that could no longer support its weight. His left leg was weak and wasted, but for the first time in his life Conn felt the wholeness that comes only to the person who is at peace with God.

When you face death, either personally or with someone you love, you are never the same. Conn and I realized our values were completely wrong, and for a little while we were closer than we had ever been, both as a couple and as a family. His work, which had become his god, was put in its place, and we began to reevaluate our priorities. We began to go to church religiously (if you will pardon the expression) to try to show God how grateful we were for all he had done in giving Conn new strength and wholeness. We spent time with the girls. We resolved to be better people in every way, but it seemed the harder we tried the more we saw our shortcomings and failures, and the more impossible the task of improvement was. I had no way of knowing then that a person cannot simply change himself permanently for the better, no matter how great his motivation. Only God can change us when we invite Him to come into our lives and do what He wants to do. Nobody told me that, and for the next several years I was to go on one long personal-improvement binge that only led to more and more frustration.

After Conn became well again he went back into construction; but his strength was still limited for a time, and so he went to work in the office of a company that hired him as soon as the doctor gave his approval. He had learned the field work well; now God was giving him the opportunity to learn the role of management. It was a difficult transition for Conn; he had always loved to work outdoors doing hard physical labor. The timing, however, was perfect. There was no way he could do the hard work now, so he was content to learn the inside of the business. He learned quickly. In less than a year he was ready to form his own company in northern California. We moved there in the spring of 1958, and Conn built the first of several homes for our family.

His business grew and prospered; indeed, for a very long time it seemed he could do nothing wrong. In an astonishingly short time he had a large corporation going, and if I had thought his work was his top priority before, it had now become his life and his god. There was no stopping him from spending every waking moment running the business and every resting moment thinking about it.

I was becoming more and more frustrated about our life together. Something had gone terribly wrong, and I had no way of knowing what had happened or how to change it for the better. I was tense and tired and angry with the girls. I watched them show the effects of living with an unpredictable mother. Daily I promised myself I would change and be what they needed; daily I watched myself fail again. While Conn was becoming more and more of a success, I was becoming a wretched failure. When I asked Conn if he would spend more time with us and share his life with us more, he looked at me angrily and said, "Don't you realize I am doing all this for you and the girls? After all, it takes a lot of money to live the way we do!" I had no answer for that. I only knew that somehow we had exchanged a standard of living for a standard of life, and I was deeply afraid for all of us.

The years slipped by. We built a second house, much grander than the first—perfect, it seemed, in every detail, except that we who occupied it were becoming less and less of a family. I decided the blame for this whole fiasco must somehow be mine, and I determined more than ever to improve myself. Thus began my self-improvement era that was to continue for years.

There was the year of "personal appearance improvement." Surely if I looked all right on the outside it would change the awfulness I knew was on the inside. For a low starting fee of one hundred dollars, I went to a modeling school for their basic course. I must emphasize *basic*, because it turned out there was a lot more to the course than the initial tuition. There was the makeup to buy (and of course, you did have to use *their* makeup in order to achieve true beauty), the coordinated wardrobe, the color analysis, the hair styling, the exercise machines, the special diets, *ad infinitum*. The cost began to rapidly rival the national debt, and in spite of all the outward improvements, I found I still had the same old problems. Now they were all slightly compounded by wondering how in the world I was ever going to pay for everything and still justify the investment, not to mention the time away from home! The old me still looked in the mirror at the new me and mockingly reminded me that in spite of it all I was still critical, frightened, lonely, and an angry wife and mother. Scratch the personal improvement. It seemed to work for some of my friends, but obviously it did not do anything for me.

In the middle of my self-improvement days two more children joined our household: Nancy, our fourth daughter, and Jonathan, a blond, blue-eyed boy we adopted, and whom we discovered was completely normal except that he grew up thinking everyone had five mothers!

Then there was the year of "returning to college." Maybe if I had a degree or two after my name it would really make me a worthy person. I started to attend classes in San Jose and found that freshmen are considerably smarter when they are fresh out of high school than when they are in their middle thirties, and that classes are still fairly routine and a little bit dull, in the first two years at least. A sudden emergency operation in the middle of a December night and the resulting long convalescence put an end to my campus days before they really got a good start.

Together, Conn and I built another new home, and it was gorgeous. Built on the brow of a hill in a community called Monte Sereno, it was a perfect home for a big family. Below the house, in a hollow on the common green that surrounded all the homes in the area, we built a boarding and training stable for show horses, and I was given the position of manager. I was highly motivated to succeed at that one; we had a lot of money invested in it to encourage me! Months went by before we finally got it filled with the right horses and riders. By the time that was accomplished, I was being torn apart by seeing the children come home each day to an empty house and by trying constantly to find a reliable, capable baby-sitter for Jon, who was still an infant. It was obvious to me that there was no way I could be in two places at one time, and yet more and more I was torn with guilt and resentment at what seemed to be a really impossible situation. The harder I tried, the guiltier I felt and the more wretched I became. I wasn't working out very well as a career woman either.

We tried religion. It had been such a good trip for a while after Conn's polio, and I thought surely there must be something there if I only tried harder. We hardly ever missed a church service and we became more and more active. Granted, as the children grew older it became

35

much harder to convince them of the worth of our weekly hassles. That was perfectly understandable when you realize that during all of their formative years Conn and I had our best arguments on the way to church.

It was always the same routine. I got up earlier on Sunday than I did the rest of the week in order to try to get things organized to a degree, so we wouldn't have our usual Sunday morning chaos. Don't ask me why it was always worse on Sunday, but the morning usually started out badly and deteriorated remarkably fast. After fifteen years of bedlam, one would think I would have given up in sheer exhaustion. But I am really stubborn about some things, and since I suspected that all this was somehow due to my own disorganization I was forever optimistic that at some point I would happen upon the right solution through sheer perseverance.

An hour and a half before "C Hour," the moment when we had to leave for church or be late, I would rout the first of the children out of bed, starting with the oldest and working down—and I do mean working! There was nothing easy about getting anyone out of bed. I would get breakfast on the table and while Conn and the older girls were eating, I would wake Jon and Nancy (if they had not already been awakened by the commotion and protests of the rest of the group) and get them ready for breakfast and baths. By that time, approximately forty-five minutes before blast-off time, I would have stopped three impending murders, a couple of larcenies ("Mom, Beck has stolen my blouse!"), and a couple of potential suicides, at least one of them my own.

Since no one in the house, with the possible exception of Conn, was particularly enchanted by the idea of the morning's activities, there was much creativity in coming up with new ideas why one child or another should not attend the services that day. The reasons covered a wide range—from a Sunday school teacher who was really weird (turned out it was my class they were talking about), to a major plague that could possibly strike that very morning in *our own church,* to a possible snowstorm that would keep us from ever returning home again. Since our California-raised children had rarely seen a blizzard, I thought that one was quite memorable—we went to church anyway.

Conn, in the meantime, had leisurely gotten out of bed (after sleeping a good hour longer than I), taken a long shower, and dressed himself with great care. After that he read the Sunday newspaper while he ate the breakfast I had prepared. At that point, while I was jamming on my hat—yes, I had learned how to put one on in the personal-improvement course, but survival is a stronger instinct than being gorgeous—and throwing a roast in the oven for dinner after church, Conn contributed his only help of the day. He would go out to the garage, start the car, and honk the horn to remind me it was time to go! I came to hate the sound of that horn with a passion, and after a while I tried to somehow get ready before he could press the button. But haste on my part only resulted in burned fingers from the oven or a hatpin poked into my head.

The atmosphere in the car was icy, to say the least, on the way to church. I would tell Conn, as quietly but firmly as I knew how, that he was completely useless when it came to getting anyone ready for church, and that he was terribly rude with that blasted horn. He would answer just as quietly (we knew, you see, that children should not be subjected to parental disagreement; I'm still not sure who we thought we were kidding!) that I was disorganized to the point of being ridiculous, and I was also hypercritical and jealous. We were both right, but that only made both of us more angry and did nothing to change the situation, and the argument continued as long as we were in the car. The moment we got to the church parking lot, however, we stepped out of the car, smiled graciously at those around us, agreed with them that it was indeed a beautiful day and that Sunday certainly was the best day of the week, and walked into the church, looking for all the world like everyone else in the crowd.

The children lost their wonder at that transformation early in life. They knew by the time they were five years old that the argument would be exactly the same the next Sunday and the next Sunday and all the rest of the Sundays for the rest of their lives. They could do nothing at all about it, except try not to get caught in the cross fire. As they grew older and wiser, however, they began to find better and more reasonable excuses for not going with us, and by the time they were in their teens they were not only adept at good excuses, but they were also totally opposed to church in any form. What good had it ever done their parents? In the end, I was forced to agree with them a thousand times over. Religion, I thought, was no answer to anything. If anything, it only compounded one's problems. If Jesus was indeed the answer, as I heard people say now and then, I certainly somehow had never found the right questions.

Early in 1966, I stood in the middle of the living room in our Monte Sereno home and took stock of my situation. The house was perfect. Below me, in the valley, I could see the lights of San Jose and San Francisco beyond that. Conn had taken enormous pride in building the house, and it was filled with lovely extras that only a contractor thinks about. The lovely foyer opened to the fifty-foot-long living room with a huge wall of glass at one end. A beautiful curving wall of paneled rosewood circled the curving staircase. Those stairs seemed to be suspended in air and were a masterpiece of engineering beauty. It was a perfect house, exquisitely furnished—and it was the emptiest house I had ever seen.

Was there anything I hadn't tried? The personal improvement didn't work; religion was for the birds; I wasn't a good career woman; I had flopped as a wife; ditto as a mother. But worst of all I had failed myself. I believed there must have been some potential there sometime, but now all I could see was a woman who could not do anything right. I wondered if maybe I was losing my mind. Surely anyone who could not be happy with all I had must have something pretty drastically wrong with her. Would my life always seem so meaningless and empty?

3

Encounter of Another Kind

Although I felt I was a failure in a lot of ways in those long years, I did prove to be a very skillful actress. Because I was doing what people have done before I was born and will continue to do after I die, no one realized the state I was in. I was acting out a role in my daily life, attempting to portray the person I believed those people around me thought I should be, and I was so successful at it that few people outside our home were aware of my poor self-image.

In the stable I was the perfect public-relations woman, constantly giving the impression of concern and discipline for the riders there. I rarely let on to anyone how anxious I was about my own children coming home to an empty house, and certainly no one guessed that the perfectly matched Mr. and Mrs. Bauer had a marriage that was coming apart at the seams!

In the years since, I have found that I am aware when women are playing roles. I can spot them quickly. A terrifically high number of women, both Christian and non-Christian, are giving Academy Award performances every day of their lives and never receiving so much as a round of applause for them! Our pride matches our determination to be either what we think others believe we are or what we want them to think about us. My life reached its lowest point, however, when a good friend of mine—a woman a little younger than I with three small children and a very successful contractor husband—went quietly into her garage one day and shot herself in the head with her husband's gun. No one seemed to understand how she possibly could have done it. With a terrible fear, I *knew* why she had! But I pretended as much ignorance as anyone else; I dared not even give words to my horror, fearful that somehow in admitting it I might just be tempted to do the same thing.

If there were a God, I often thought, would He allow such an existence as mine? Could He possibly be that cruel and tormenting? I went to a pastor I knew and asked how you could be sure you were a Christian. With slightly more passion and warmth than ecclesiastically necessary, he patted me on the knee, said I was surely as good a Christian as anyone in his church, and offered to counsel with me as much as I wanted. I thanked him and left, realizing that if he meant what I thought he probably meant, I would only be adding guilt to the rest of my problems.

Then one day, a few months after we had moved into the new house in Monte Sereno, I heard the news that a friend and her family had moved back into our area after an absence of several years. Conn and I had known Jack and Nell Chinchen many years before when we had all lived in Santa Clara. Like us, they had been very active in the church there, but their attitude had been definitely different from ours. They actually had seemed to be doing what they did because they really wanted to, not because they had felt any compulsion or need for recognition, as was the case with us. Wonder of wonders, they actually had seemed to enjoy it!

After a time, they left Santa Clara, their beautiful home, and his very good executive position to attend a seminary with the idea of becoming missionaries. Jack's grandfather was the head of a huge corporation, one of the largest in the nation, and Jack was in line for his position as chairman of the board. And yet, as we attended farewell parties given for them, I got the distinct impression that neither of them felt they were giving up anything; rather, they seemed sure they were gaining everything! It didn't make any sense to me, and Conn's explanation was that they had become real fanatics.

Now they were back in town. Impulsively, I called Nell one evening at their newly rented home, and asked if they could stop by sometime and visit us. I used the excuse that I wanted them to see our new home and get caught up on all that had been happening in our lives in the years since Santa Clara. Actually, they had been on my mind a hundred times through the years and I felt I had to find out, if I could only ask the right questions, what in the world had made their church experiences so different from ours.

It was late in the evening when they stopped by, and as Nell stepped into the light of the living room she was no longer the fashion plate I had remembered from years before. Her hair had become rather gray and her dress was mediocre and a little out of style. But as she came closer, across the foyer and down the long room, I was aware of the most remarkable glow on her face and sparkle in her eyes. I was suddenly overwhelmed with the thought that for one of the first times in my life, I was seeing a woman who was really enjoying peace of mind. And I also knew, with a physical agony, that I had been searching for that peace all along, and that without it I would never really be alive.

I was back to square one on the questions, though. How could I ask her why she looked so peaceful? If she laughed at that question I knew I would feel too foolish to bear it, and so instead we talked of unimportant things—their house, our house, how our children were growing up, Conn's business. And then the conversation began to change. They began to tell us of their church in Washington. When we asked the secret of the remarkable growth the church had experienced during the years they had served there, they said quite simply that everyone involved in the church had a personal relationship with God. I couldn't remember ever hearing that term in my life, up to that point. But I dared not show my ignorance, especially since the other three, including Conn, seemed to use the words so freely.

I said rather shakily that I really thought such a relationship must be just a little idealistic and unattainable, but they assured me quickly that it was not at all. I asked how they could *know* that people knew God personally. Jack answered my question. He said he supposed that one of the ways it happened was through their Bible classes where people came to know about the relationship and wanted it for themselves. Trying hard not to appear too eager, I asked Nell why she didn't start a Bible class here in town. I said I had a lot of friends who probably would love it.

A few weeks later she did start that Bible class, and I never missed a single session. We started the study in the Gospel of John, and as we worked our way through that book I gradually began to understand—as if someone had turned on a light—that here was a God who had not just created a world and a helpless people, but who was the Someone actually personally interested in those He created. Here was a God who did not help those who helped themselves, but a loving Father who was willing to help those who *couldn't* help themselves! For the first time in thirty-four years, I could stop trying to improve myself and help myself, and simply be me. It seemed far too good to be true. I was a little afraid at first that perhaps Nell was wrong about this; it seemed far too simple. But she spoke with such authority!

It took quite a while, but the longer we studied together the more I knew beyond a shadow of a doubt that I had finally found the answer I had been searching for. And when, in June of 1966, I knelt and asked Him to come into my life and be forever my Savior and my Lord, He came. To my joy and astonishment I knew He had come, not because of an emotional experience but because He said He would in His own Word. And I knew that the authority with which Nell spoke was not because she was my teacher, but because she was simply repeating what God Himself had said.

Nell continued to teach our Bible class for the next year and a half, and although I can't remember all the lessons we learned, I remember two of them very well, and they changed my life.

Time and again I called Nell on the phone with the desperate question, "What shall I do in this situation?" Her answer never varied, and it never failed to make me angry. Instead of telling me the answer I knew she absolutely must have, her reply was invariably, "Clare, let's just pray about it and see what God would have you do." It seemed so hard to wait and take a chance that perhaps God would not hear and answer at all. But He never failed.

God was faithful, and Nell was a whale of a good teacher. She knew that every time God answered a prayer, my own faith would be strengthened, and she was so right. To this day I am eternally grateful that she was willing to share with me the privilege of growing.

The other lesson Nell constantly stressed was that we must use the faith God gives us, no matter how small it seems, or He will not provide us with more. That wisdom came to a phenomenal test after a year and a half when Nell called me one day and said she had something to ask of me. Of course I would have done anything for her, and I told her, boldly, to ask away; her wish was my command! I knew the Chinchens were leaving San Jose, having been called to a church in Mississippi, and that

45

they had prayed with everyone else in the class for a new teacher of God's choice. But when Nell announced that day that she believed God wanted *me* to teach the class, I nearly fainted with fear.

I didn't think Nell could possibly have heard God wrong. but I also didn't think God had that good a sense of humor! After all, there were twenty women in that class, and nearly every one of them had been a Christian longer than I. To top it off, there were at least two pastor's wives in the group. I promised Nell that I would at least pray about it, and I spent the next several days in a fog, not really knowing *how* to pray yet wanting more than anything to really know God's will in this whole ridiculous thing. There were, it seemed to me, so many other women who were really *qualified* to teach. I alternated between laughing and crying.

I finally prayed the simplest of prayers, asking God to make me willing to be His teacher if that was what He wanted for me, but I reminded Him fervently that if any teaching was to be done, He would have to do it. He knew I loved Him and that I wanted to share that love with everyone I came in contact with. More than anything else I wanted to be His woman, and if that meant becoming a teacher, then so be it.

I called Nell back and told her of my conversation with God, and that I was willing to teach but she had to promise to pray for me constantly. She wasn't even surprised. She just said, with her lovely southern accent, "Oh Clare, you are going to enjoy it so!"

How right she was!

Within the next year my life was literally transformed. The teaching was not easy; it was definitely a gift from God, but I had to study like mad to stay an inch ahead of my students. The class was not the only exciting place in my life. As my children watched God change me from an angry, frustrated, fearful woman, they wanted to know why. I told them as simply as I could that I had asked Jesus to come into my life and that He was changing me into what He wanted me to be. And changing me He was.

The children and Conn did not see perfection, and still have not, I fear, but the softening, gentle hand of God was visible in my life. Julie said that when she came down to breakfast the third morning in a row and I still wasn't angry or uptight, she knew some kind of a miracle had taken place! Miracle of miracles, some order began to come into my life. Conn began to encourage me to draw up lists and priorities. As my lists began to grow, my frustration began to shrink, and the children, who were the beneficiaries, began to blossom in the atmosphere of an orderly, calm home.

I read about Hannah Wesley with her fifteen children, and asked God to help me find time for each one of my five. He did, and I found I not only liked them as individuals, but they began to like me, too. You are required to love your parents, but it takes a very special act of God to make you like them. They watched and they wondered, and before many months had passed they wanted to share in the miracle. One by one they asked Christ to come into their lives, too.

Conn was considerably more stubborn about seeing or admitting or enjoying the changes he was experiencing along with the rest of us. He had always been the unchallenged leader in our home, and he was more than a little upset that I was apparently enjoying a world in which he was not a part. More and more he fought the growing conviction that his relationship with God had deteriorated completely from that interminable night in San Bernardino Hospital so long ago. That night he had asked God to save him and had promised to be His man. After all, he reasoned to me in some of the increasingly rare conversations we were now sharing, he had done very well on his own, and if he came to God now He would probably ask something impossible of him to see if he really meant business. Could Conn give up all he had worked for and surrender it all to God? No way! For an agonizingly long time Conn fought a silent but fierce battle against God's gentle pressure.

In December, six months after the pressure started for Conn, he found he was helplessly faced with impending financial disaster. The business he had built with such pride and determination was faced with bankruptcy, and in hopeless despair Conn realized he had not done so very well with his own plan for his life. Two days before Christmas, at four in the morning, Conn knelt in the living room and asked God to take over his life and make him the man He wanted him to be.

It turned out that God didn't want the business at all. He wanted Conn! And with his capitulation to God, Conn faced the financial problems with a new determination to do whatever could be done to solve the problems in an honorable way. For him, bankruptcy was not an honorable alternative. With some tremendously hard work, some considerable power from God, and a helpful banker who changed his mind about calling in one of the very large notes that was due the first of January, the business did not fail. It not only survived the slump, but was stronger and more viable by the next summer than it had ever been before.

The years of teaching were exciting for me—it is common knowledge that the teacher always learns more than her students. And God, in love, did not allow me to teach anything He had not already taught me, sometimes the hard way.

I learned, for instance, that if you are to teach others about God's priorities you must first have your own priorities straight. I continued to work at the stable for a while after I became a Christian, but more and more I knew I had to be at home, available to both Jon and the

48

girls, and Conn as well—when they needed me, not just when they managed to fit into my schedule! Conn and I began to pray for a manager for the barn. That was not an easy prayer for me to pray, by the way. I had a very real and vested interest in the stable. And I wasn't at all certain that anyone else could really do as good a job as I could.

With His usual class, however, God chose a man for us. Bob Thompson, one of the best stable managers, horse trainers, and equestrians in the country, came to work for us. By some miracle of coincidence—divine, I decided emphatically—Bob's stable was sold out from under him as a home developer bought the land for houses, and Bob was suddenly available to work with us. He was the one person in the world to whom I could easily hand over the stable, but the very one I had not dared to pray for. He was too good! How often, I wonder, does God want to bless us beyond our wildest dreams, and we stubbornly refuse to give Him the pleasure of hearing us ask.

We looked at Jesus in the Bible class, and then we looked at ourselves. I realized He had a very long way to go not only to make my character conform to His but to make it acceptable and beautiful to me as well. You see, I knew me from the inside out, and while I could fool others once in a while, I could never fool me. But God knew all about me, and gently, and with the greatest love, He began to change me as I was able to bear it.

One day, after returning from a Thanksgiving vacation with Conn's sister, Elaine, and her family in Denver, I was made nakedly aware that I lied as easily as I brushed my teeth, and with about that much planning.

Julie and Beck were in high school; Lisa was in junior high. As we flew to Denver they told me that when we got home from the vacation I would have to write them excuses saying they had been ill. That way they could make up the work they missed without penalty. An unexcused absence meant they would have to take a zero for the days missed.

Now they were all very good students, and taking the zeroes would not have hurt their final grade point average in the least, but they simply assumed I would write the excuses as I always had. Perhaps you will understand that this was a habit of such long standing that neither the request nor my answer of yes caused me even a moment of concern. Lying about little things had become a way of life.

We returned home, and on Monday they reminded me about writing the excuses. Hastily I wrote the notes to excuse each one "because she was ill." Suddenly, for the very first time in years, I was acutely uncomfortable about telling a lie. I reassured myself that I was not really lying about it; after all, they had all caught colds in the mountain snow of Denver. But as I hastily put on some makeup before driving them to school, I looked in the mirror and thought to myself, "So that's what a liar looks like!"

Pushing the thought out of my mind, I drove them to school. I tried to forget the incident, but found I simply could not. As I tried to pray I remembered that God hates a liar. "Curses!" I said, "Everyone is a liar part of the time." *Not if they are mine,* God gently replied! I tried to study my Bible, and every place I looked it seemed to scream, "Confess your sin, untruthful one!"

For three days I tried to bargain with God with no success whatsoever. *The damage is done, Lord. There's nothing I can do about it now, you see. You do understand, don't you, Lord?* Maybe He did, but I didn't. Finally, I gave up. I decided that all I could do was write a note to the dean of women at the high school and tell her what I had done and why I had to make it right. The note, when I finally got it written, was a masterpiece of brevity.

"Dear Mrs. Wilson: The other day I wrote you a note asking you to excuse my two daughters from a recent absence because they were ill. That was not true. We had gone on a family vacation. I am so sorry I lied to you. I became a Christian about a year ago, and I find that I must be honest because of my God. I hope you will forgive me."

It was a hard note to write, but once it was done I had an even more difficult job ahead of me. Julie and Beck had stayed up until nearly midnight for several days making up the work, and now I had to tell them it was all for nothing. Because of my sin, they had worked for credit that would not be given to them.

I have found that one of the reasons parents do not apologize to their children more often is that it is very humbling. The other reason is that children are not always extremely graceful at receiving apologies. As I shared with the girls the content of the note, I saw first disbelief and then undisguised dismay come over their faces. "Do you mean we've done this all for *nothing?*" Beck roared, her pencil poised above her work in a dagger-like position. Julie was older and slightly more subtle. "Now, Mom, you have to do what you think is right, of course, but I do hope you didn't plan on my taking that note into Mrs. Wilson's office, because I am not. You wrote it—you deliver it."

Ungrateful child! If that was supposed to be the coup de grace, it almost was. I had simply assumed that she would be glad to do that little thing for me, and somehow the rascal had read my mind and refused before I had a decent chance to issue the order. I told her that of course I had no intention of having her do my dirty work for me (lying still came surprisingly easy in moments of great trauma), and I left the room to ask God how in the world I was going to get that thing to the school. His unbelievable answer was to take it myself. In person. Face to face. Good night! How low did I have to get? There was nothing else to do; I had gone this far with it and I knew I might as well finish the job.

Morning came, and since I had not died in the night (which would have been the easy way out), I prepared to face what was bound to be a pretty sad situation at the very best. The worst thing they could do, I thought, was throw the girls out of school and print my picture in the paper as the liar of the week.

I got Jon ready to go and together we went out to the garage and climbed into the car. A storm had started in the night and it was raining furiously. I got there safely and then spent the next twenty minutes sogging along in the rain, trying to find the right building in the midst of all the construction going on at the high school.

Jon was howling with indignation and I looked like a drowned cat by the time we reached the dean's office. I simply laid the note down on her desk and waited for the ax to fall. She said not a word as she read it, but when I looked at her she started to smile. I think she would have laughed out loud had she been just a little less professional, but all she said was, "Mrs. Bauer, I have been in this office for seventeen years. In that time I have received literally thousands of excuses, and most of them were probably not true. You are the first one who ever admitted writing one. Congratulations. That must be some God you have!"

I floated out of the office and found my car on the very first try. Jon fell asleep as we drove home, and I thanked God for being so gracious as He taught me a very hard lesson. I want you to know that when I taught my class the next week about being honest women, it was remarkably effective!

The girls, incidentally, were given the credit for their work at school, and I didn't, thank God, make the front page of the paper. To this day, however, I find it is still very easy for me to lie. But the consequences are invariably too great to consider, and God is always willing to give me the strength to be an honest woman—when I ask for it. It is a great thing to be able to look in the mirror these days and know I can trust that woman who looks back at me, not because she is a pillar of honesty but because she has a very honest God.

Then there was the lesson on communication. Communication is not like riding a bicycle, I have found. Once you know how to ride a bike it is never an effort again. But in our family I find we have to work at communication constantly. Once Christ came to live at our house, communication became much easier and more genuine, and our conversations became salted with love and understanding. But we all had to work at it.

When our third daughter, Lisa, was about thirteen or fourteen years old, she stopped sharing things with the rest of the family. Very effectively and efficiently she built a wall of silence around herself and her activities. It frightened me, but no matter how I tried to help her come back into the family emotionally, nothing seemed to work. Good communication, like the tango, takes two, and she was just plain not interested. She decided on this particular form of rebellion, and I want you to know it was extremely effective! The less she was willing to talk to us, the more earnestly I began to talk to God about her, pleading with Him to show me how to break down that wall of silence and hostility and to start exchanging thoughts and worlds again.

Nothing happened to change the condition for months, until one morning, after I had about given up hope that we would ever really understand Lisa again. On that memorable day she came down the stairs and casually asked if I still got up early in the morning to pray.

Early in my Christian life I had gotten into the habit of praying and enjoying God very early in the morning. There was nothing particularly significant about the early hour; it is just that I have learned through the years that that was one of the few times I could depend on the house being quiet, without either children or telephone demanding my attention. Also, it is very easy for me to get up early. I never last until midnight, but I am bright-eyed and bushy-tailed at six in the morning.

With more than a little curiosity, I answered her that yes, indeed, I still did get up at that hour to pray. To my complete surprise she asked if I minded if she joined me.

"Mind?" I said. "I'd be delighted!"

On second thought I added, "But honey, that is really very early for you, and if you decide in the morning you'd rather not, I will understand."

Now mind you, God had handed me this opportunity on a silver platter and here I was giving her a way out! I can't tell you how often I've done that through the years. But God is faithful, and when He is ready to give a gift He usually persists. The next morning, almost before I was out of bed, down the stairs came Lisa. We talked for a little while, really sharing for the first time in months, and then we prayed together. As we continued that for the next two years, we found we were able to say things to God that we absolutely couldn't say to each other without a lot of anger and tears. I began to see her world from her point of view and she began to understand my concerns. We both did a lot of growing.

Today I consider Lisa one of my dearest friends, and we have a rare understanding between us. It all started in those early morning prayer sessions that God initiated for us in answer to a plea for honest communication.

There were a thousand other lessons through the years

that God taught me. I shared the things I learned with the Bible classes, which had grown to two a week and involved more than a hundred women. Together we watched God change the lives of women and their families. I got a special kind of joy from watching the women of my neighborhood receive Christ. They had seen our family change and were intrigued by what they observed. Two of these women were special, because of all the families in Monte Sereno, theirs had seemed so perfect, even without God. They had almost everything one could possibly ask for.

Linda lived down the hill from us. Her marriage to Bill seemed not only secure but extremely happy. Their oldest child, Christopher, soon became Jon's bosom buddy. Together they took swimming lessons, went to nursery school, cut each other's hair with my pinking shears, and in general were the very best of friends.

Linda and I visited often together during the day, and we included each other at our parties and gatherings. Their family life fascinated me because, although they were quite religious in a conventional way, attending church two or three times a month, they really appeared to have very little time for God in their everyday lives. I asked Linda to come to the Bible class several times, but each time there was always a good excuse why she could not come. Eventually I stopped asking her. During one of our rare conversations about spiritual things, I knew we were simply talking in two different languages. While Linda was far too polite to dismiss it, I finally got the idea that she was totally uninterested and felt no need whatsoever for a relationship with God. But I loved her for herself, and so, although it really hurt not to be able to talk about the things that meant the most to me, I asked God for the grace to enjoy her just as she was. He truly gave it to me; she was a dear friend. But I was genuinely surprised when one day, when our friendship was about six years old, Linda asked if she could ride along with me when I spoke at a Christian Women's Club luncheon in nearby Atherton. Thinking she did not really understand what I would be talking about, I gave her every opportunity I could think of to back out. She didn't take a single one of them, and on the day of the luncheon she called and reminded me to pick her up so she could go along.

On our way home from the luncheon, Linda told me that during the invitation to ask Christ into one's life, she had asked Him to come into her life and do what He wanted with her. I was so surprised that I could not find a word to say in reply, and so she continued. "I've been watching your life change for six years, Clare, and I've come to the conclusion I need what you have."

My first reaction was, "Oh, dear, Lord, if I had known she was watching I probably would have been much more careful in *all* my actions!"

Linda and Bill have experienced some terrifically difficult times in their personal lives in the past few years, but their faith in God has grown richer and deeper with each difficulty. In a recent letter to me, she said that without God her life would not have been merely unbearable; she probably would have had a complete breakdown! But because He is there she knows she can weather the storms. Although His presence does not necessarily make life easy, it does give both Linda and Bill tremendous hope—and that, my friends, makes all the difference in the world.

Another woman in our neighborhood was tall, beautiful, slender Pat. She was the envy of every woman in the area, and one we all knew had her act together in the best possible way. Her home was one of the nicest in an area of very nice homes. Her children were bright and attractive and her doctor husband was not only handsome but brilliant as well. Who could ask for more than that? Pat could.

Pat had everything you could ask for in a material way but nothing at all emotionally or spiritually. Like Linda, Pat and her family were religious, but they gained nothing from it. Pat's husband was a perfectionist, which is exactly what one wants from a doctor but is more than a little difficult to live with in a partner.

I was drawn to Pat as I had been to Linda. She was so much of what I had wanted to be before I met Jesus and could accept myself as I was. But the longer I talked to Pat, the more convinced I became that the act we all thought she had so well together was just that—an act—and it wasn't really together at all.

I shared with Pat a dozen times the changes Christ had brought into my life, and one day she asked Christ into her life. The changes were remarkable.

Pat and her husband still live in that lovely home in Monte Sereno, and it is still one of the nicest ones around. Her husband is still a doctor, brilliant enough that when someone in my family has problems in his particular specialty we want to go that extra thousand miles to consult him, not as our friend but as a doctor. But he too has changed. As he watched Pat change, Chuck was attracted to Christ and eventually invited Him into his life, and now his life too reflects God's power and love. Their children are as attractive and bright as before (and I suspect as mischievous), but now they are secure and confident in a way they were not before their parents came to know Christ. Oh yes, it is a very different home now. Love and joy absolutely radiate from the walls!

I was teaching about the husband's headship of the home in the spring of 1974, and it was with mixed emotions that I shared with the women that since my husband was the head of our home, I would no longer be teaching the Bible class in the fall. We would be moving to Idaho. ("What is an Idaho?" some of them asked.) I am so grateful that I did not have to make the decision to leave California. Once I was willing to give God the freedom to lead Conn, and then to joyfully follow his leading, I was able to look forward to the move and the old house and the wretched weather.

4

The Spring of '76

Idaho is a state of extremes. The winters, which last from November to May in a normal year, are long and cold. Sudden blizzards whip out of the southwest with the fury and paralyzing force of an enraged grizzly bear. Mounting snow piles twenty feet high in the mountains surrounding the valley and the snow-covered valley becomes a child's wonderland, a sportsman's paradise, and a housebound mother's prison.

When we returned to Idaho after spending twenty years in sunny California, what I dreaded most were the long, bitter winters. (I am so easily chilled that I have been known to get frostbite when hunting for the lettuce in the refrigerator!) The idea of voluntarily moving back to such a climate struck me as one of the last signs of total mental breakdown.

But seasons do change and come to an end, and eventually the winter subsides and gives way to the thawing winds of spring, called the Chinook. There is a song that sings of the silver-white winters that melt into spring, but I realized our very first year in Idaho that the key word in that phrase is not silver-white, as I had always thought; it is *melt!* The snow turns from white to ugly to mud; the road becomes a sea of mire; and the alternate freezing and thawing that continues for weeks invariably causes people to wonder aloud if spring is ever going to come. I had only to live here a very short time before I realized,

59

with a touch of desperation that bordered on despair, that that *was* spring! Like a giant who awakens slowly and with great irritation from his long winter slumber, the land reluctantly begins to come alive. And then, quite suddenly it always seems, it is June.

Almost as if they are in tune with an invisible but very accurate calendar, the lilac bushes burst into bloom, their purple flowers filling the air with their unforgettable perfume. The tulips and daffodils smile at the sun in their ridiculously bright dresses, the apple trees adorn themselves in delicate pink and green seemingly overnight, and lo! winter is past.

June of 1976 came like that. I walked slowly through the yard the first week of the month, wondering why it all looked so bright and fresh and green to me again, as it had the spring before. Whatever the reason, I thanked God for eyes to see such beauty.

Several months before, I had listened to a woman speak at a Christian Woman's Club luncheon about a personal improvement course she had developed. When I first heard of the topic I wasn't the least bit interested—I had been that route. I had found that the vast majority of personal improvement courses do nothing at all for the individual except change her outward appearance. I know from personal experience that making only the outer woman more acceptable can really cause the inner woman more problems than ever. I mentally marked that luncheon off the calendar. I would wait another month and see if they could come up with something that was a little more relevant to my life.

At almost the last minute, a friend called from another town on the CWC circuit and said she wanted me to hear this woman speak. "This gal is really different, Clare," she said, "and I just know you will love what she has to say."

I had to admit that some of the women I had met in Idaho could do with a little personal improvement. Reluctantly I decided to blow the afternoon and drive the forty miles to hear this speaker. To my surprise, I not only enjoyed what she had to say, but I thought for the first time that maybe there was some hope for personal improvement after all. The difference between this course and other courses I had heard about was that it not only concentrated on the outer woman, but it largely emphasized a relationship with Christ for the inner woman. The combination makes a woman totally beautiful! I surely hoped some woman in our area would decide to teach that course.

That night I shared with Conn what I had learned, and his response surprised and dismayed me a little. He wanted me to write to the woman about getting a franchise to teach the course in our area. Somewhat reluctantly I began to consider it. Within a few months I had the franchise and my firsty forty students.

The course consisted of eight three-hour lessons, one per week. Since there were too many students for one class, and the women had different needs regarding hours, I taught two classes at night and two during the morning hours. Conn remodeled the two-bedroom apartment above the garage into a studio for me, and as the classes got underway I became more and more excited about their potential for the women in our area of Idaho.

The first class was on posture and facial expression. My students were eager to learn and receptive to all the information, and I was greatly encouraged.

The second class was on diet and exercise, and we had a lot of fun with that one.

The third had been one of my favorites, and it was the main reason I had decided to teach the course. It concerns personality and self-acceptance, the basis being a relationship with the Lord Jesus Christ. There is no way a woman can be truly beautiful if Christ is not the center of her life. The teacher gives each student an opportunity to ask Christ to come into her life if she has never done so. Even women who had been Christians for a long time told me their relationship with God became even more precious to them as they realized how unique and special they are to God. Three women told me they had invited Christ to come into their lives for the first time. At that point I knew the classes were worth every bit of work and time I put into them, even if nobody learned another thing!

The fourth class was even more popular than the first three. Almost every woman I know wants to look her best in her clothes and to know how to plan her wardrobe. We covered that thoroughly in the three-hour class, and then arranged for each of the students to come individually on Friday the fourth of June, or Saturday the fifth, for a color analysis.

So this first weekend of June promised to be a particularly busy one. Conn would be out of town at a retreat for some of our church leaders, to be held at a resort in the mountains about fifty miles away. He left on a Friday afternoon and planned to be home late Saturday night.

Friday had been a hectic day, but it was fun. Each woman's analysis took about thirty minutes, and then she needed another thirty to forty-five minutes to organize her color samples for her notebook. At almost any given moment we had a half-dozen or more women in the studio. I was greatly enjoying myself; the women had become special to me as I came to know them. Each had added much to my life; most of them were becoming good friends. At the end of Friday I was very tired, but it was a good feeling and I had not missed Conn at all. I knew as I went to bed Friday night that the next day would be even more hectic, but I also knew I was going to thoroughly enjoy it.

Jon and Nancy were rather at loose ends on Saturday

morning. As I dashed out to the studio I called back, "Come on out to the studio as soon as you finish breakfast. I'll put you to work!"

For fifteen-year-old Nancy it was a welcome invitation. She loved the course and was excited about helping in any way she was asked. In less than fifteen minutes she arrived, dressed in shorts and a halter top and barefoot. Bare feet are not usually considered feminine and stylish, but I decided not to quench her eagerness by making her return to the house to put on her shoes.

Jon came up to the studio a little later—also dressed casually in shorts and a rather grubby-looking T-shirt, but wearing tennis shoes. I barely looked up from my work to smile at him.

"What are your plans for the day, tiger?" I asked, as if I didn't already know. He had just bought a new dirt bike with money he had borrowed from Conn. Growing fast at eleven and surprisingly strong for his size, Jon was planning to work through the summer, moving irrigation pipes on the farm to repay the loan. With his new bike in mind, I already knew his answer.

"I think I'll just mess around the yard this morning on my bike and see what she'll do," was his casual but boyishly boastful answer.

"Fine," I replied, a little distracted by the women who were fast arriving. "Would you like to call Terry or one of your other pals and go fishing on the river?"

"Maybe this afternoon, Mom. But I think I'll stick around the place this morning."

Chalk up small miracle number one. In less than three hours, anyone fishing along the Teton River would be dying or fighting desperately for life. Jon's choice to stay home that morning saved me the agonies other parents were to suffer as they frantically tried to find sons who had gone fishing that lovely June morning.

My thoughts bounced from the dangers of motorcycling to the placid river. Why did I feel a momentary relief, when the fishing was a much safer sport, for goodness sake? And then, as a finger that catches fleetingly on a snag in fabric, there flashed in my mind a composite of recently read articles from our county newspaper:

> Due to minor problems in the construction of the Teton Dam, floodgates will be opened somewhere between the 5th and the 12th of June to allow some of the reservoir water to escape. At that time, residents who live along the river may expect some insignificant flooding to occur. There is no cause for alarm.

No reason to worry. Yet I was glad when Jon decided to stay around home. I laughed a little to myself. If the river were *ever* going to spill over its banks, I thought, today would be the day. Conn and I had long ago decided it was a family tradition for things to go wrong only when he was out of town.

In a few minutes I heard the roar of the dirt bike as Jon bounced along in the pasture. I could see him in my mind's eye, ripping along faster than he should be going, putting Evel Knievel to shame as he jumped the Grand Canyon in his imagination. "Oh, God," I silently prayed, "You've kept your hand on him so faithfully and carefully for eleven years. Please don't let go of Jon today!"

For the next two hours, as the students came and went, I worked quickly and intently, trying to keep ahead of the flow of women. The time flew by and everyone was having a great time. Once, in the distance, I heard the sound of a wailing siren, a sound so foreign in Idaho that I wondered if I was really hearing it. But it quickly faded and was gone from my mind even before the sound stopped. I scarcely noticed how quickly the morning

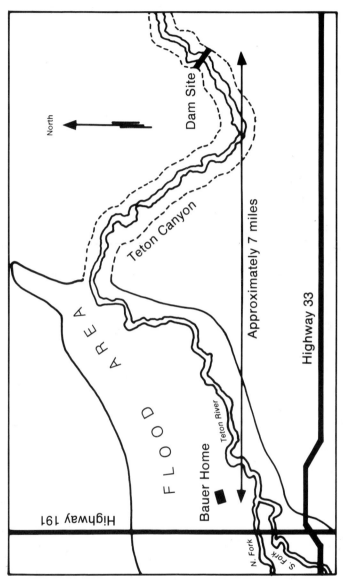

North

Dam Site

Teton Canyon

Approximately 7 miles

Highway 33

FLOOD AREA

Bauer Home

Teton River

Highway 191

N. Fork

S. Fork

Area Affected by the Teton Dam Break

The once confined Teton River now flows smoothly through the 1,000 foot wide rupture in the Teton Dam. (AP Wire Photo)

More than eighty billion gallons of water and tons of dirt and silt began pouring into the Upper Snake River Valley as the 300 foot high Teton Dam gave way on June 5, 1976. (Photo by Lynn Schwendiman of Wilford, Idaho)

The residential area of Rexburg, where daughter Julie and son-in-law Carl lived, was covered by flood waters for several days. (AP Wire Photo)

After the flood waters receded, the clean-up work began (above). By 1977, the old log house was looking better than ever (below).

had gone. My stomach began to grumble, reminding me of the time, and I realized with a start that it was nearly noon. As I paused in my work I heard someone clunking up the stairs to the studio. It had to be Jon. Surely none of my students would dare walk with such a heavy tread!

"How soon's lunch?" was his impatient question.

"Just as soon as I finish doing Yvonne and Susan. How about jumping on your bike and getting the mail for me while you wait?"

The delight in his dark blue eyes was electric. I could read his mind. At last! Permission—no, an order—to ride on the lane, when he had always been restricted to ride in the considerably safer, but much bumpier pasture. The lane consisted of hard-packed gravel and would allow more speed. I sighed. It wouldn't do the least bit of good to say it, but my mother instincts won out over the facts and I called to his fleeting back, "Don't ride too fast, son!"

"Sure, Mom," came floating back up the stairs. Sure, my heart echoed. Another three gray hairs—all of them named Jon, as usual.

Almost before I could get started again with my last two students for the morning, in what I *knew* was not a reasonable time to ride the quarter-mile to the mail box and back, I heard Jon's bike come to a screeching stop at the garage. Annoyed because I was aware that he must have ridden far too fast for safety, I angrily turned to the door as I heard Jon come pounding up the stairs for the second time in five minutes.

He came rushing into the room. His face was white and strained and his eyes, so filled with delight only moments before, were filled with tears. Something was terribly wrong with my son!

He ran over to me, oblivious of the other women in the room, and grabbed my arm with hands so tense it frightened me. "Mom," he choked, "we've got to get out of here *right now!* The dam is broke!"

The room, which had been overflowing with laughter and women's voices, was suddenly completely silent. In the stillness I could hear not only the sound of my own breathing, but far away—as in a distant nightmare—the wailing of that siren again.

"Jon, get hold of yourself! *What* dam has broken?" I was not aware of fright. I was aware of a rigid tension suddenly filling the room, of a surprisingly angry annoyance for this rude interruption of my life and my work, of Nancy's bare feet, of the sun dappling the bright walls of the studio, of a sudden cold confusion. But not fear. Not then.

"Mom, when I got to the mailbox Nicki was throwing things into their pickup. I asked Cory what was going on and he said we've got to get out of here. The dam is breaking and we're all going to drown if we don't leave right now!"

Gradually my mind began to adjust. Nicki and Paul were our closest neighbors. Cory, their oldest child, was Jon's age and his best friend. Nicki was pregnant. She had no business lifting heavy things into a pickup, I thought.

"Now Jon, I want you to think carefully. How do they know the dam is breaking? And is it the Teton Dam you are talking about?"

Since there is no other dam in the immediate area, you probably think it was obvious which dam it was. But you have to understand that when it comes to emergency situations I stop thinking. Years ago, when the president was assassinated, someone told me Kennedy was shot and I remember asking, "Which Kennedy?" So I was only running true to form.

"How did Nicki and Cory hear the news, honey?"

"It's on the radio, Mom. They say everyone out here has to leave right now!"

The Teton Dam . . . failed? Foolishness! It was a brand new $55 million federally built dam that wasn't even finished yet. Failed? Impossible! But so what if it had? It couldn't possibly be full yet. And even if the reservoir behind the dam had been filled, how much damage could it do when there were thousands of acres of land for the water to spread out over? It would simply roar down the river bed and rise to a depth of two or three or maybe four feet if we were really unfortunate. Water in the basement, yes. Probably some damage to the newly sprouted crops in the fields. But surely there could be no need for this frightful panic I saw mirrored from Jon's face to those of the women in the studio!

Upon looking at Jon's face and hearing his words, the women in the room did not share my reaction and reasoning. They grabbed handbags and car keys and rushed for the stairs in a group. Nancy turned to me, my confusion reflected in her face. "What shall I do to help, Mom?" she asked quietly, although her face had suddenly become very pale.

"Now, Nance, don't be afraid, honey. I can't believe there is any real cause for alarm, but I don't want things with motors to get all wet and ruined. So jump into your car and drive it into town, and I'll meet you there in a little while at Rankins."

My calmness was completely misunderstood by my students, and for days afterward they talked about my courage and coolness. How little they really knew! There is nothing at all courageous about being calm in a situation one believes presents no danger, and I honestly thought there was nothing at all to fear from the water. Deliberately, as I mulled the facts over in my mind, I remembered again the notice in the paper. Of course, I thought, that explains it. Somewhere upstream, some-one had gotten a little bit wet from the overflow that had been turned loose from the dam, and hysterically had decided the dam had broken and we were all going to drown. *Chicken Little!* I thought. *The sky is falling!* At some point in the afternoon a lot of people were going to feel awfully foolish when they realized how they were taken in by a silly rumor!

I turned to Jon and spoke very gently, with my arms around him, to try to ease his awful fear.

"Now, honey, I don't think there is anything at all to be so terribly frightened about, but I want you to get on your bike and ride it down the road to the main highway. Drive very carefully, Jon, and slowly. I will follow you in my car in a couple of minutes, and pick you up shortly. I love you, Jon."

Nancy and Jon dashed out, and for a moment I was all alone in my quiet, sunny studio. I walked into the office and closed the file drawers, admiring their neatness.I glanced at the wall clock. It was just 12:15. I turned and slowly walked down the stairs into the warm noonday sun.

I got into my car and started to drive away. Realizing that I had left the door open, I went back and firmly closed the door, wondering if I should take the time to move all the bicycles in the garage upstairs to keep them dry. Deciding against it, I drove away.

I was starting to be more than a little annoyed over having to stop my whole day and rearrange my whole schedule to accommodate someone's harebrained rumor. That's one of the troubles with a small commu-nity, I told myself resentfully. Little things get blown out of proportion so fast! I drove down the lane, only to stop on impulse at Paul and Nicki's house. I ran across the lawn and into her house through the open front door.

"Nicki, I think this is really dumb," I said a little

edgily, almost as if *she* had started the rumor. "Surely the Teton Dam can't have broken!"

She looked up tiredly, and said with a great weariness, "I think you're probably right, but the radio says we have to get out." I looked at her with compassion. Only months before, she and Paul had lost their home to a fire that had come on Thanksgiving weekend, and now their new house was about to get all wet. There was just no justice at all sometimes, it seemed.

"Do you really think there is any danger?" I persisted. How I wanted her to say, "Of course not!" She didn't answer for a minute. Neither of us could possibly have known at that very moment, less than three miles away, a fifteen-foot wall of water from the broken dam was crashing down on the valley. Coming straight at the farm, carrying hundreds of tons of debris that moments before had been homes, farm buildings, and machinery, it was in effect a four-mile-wide battering ram powered by the angry, devastating Teton River. Both our homes were directly in its path, and in less than an hour Paul and Nicki's would not just get wet; it would disappear forever without a trace.

We talked a few minutes longer and agreed there was probably no real danger, except for an awful, muddy mess to clean up in the basements of the area afterward. I started to leave. Having a second thought, I turned back and asked Nicki if I could use her telephone to call Conn at the retreat. Her reply, as she heaved another chair on top of a table, was "Help yourself."

Conn had just finished an early lunch and was walking out the door of the dining hall as the call came. The manager of the lodge ran to catch him just as he was disappearing toward his conference meeting.

"Hi sweetie. How's the retreat going? Rapidly backwards, I assume?" was my greeting. (That is our standard joke about retreats.)

69

"Look, Conn," I continued, "we have just gotten a message that they are having some problems at the dam. We are supposed to evacuate the area. I can't believe that it can be terribly serious, but is there anything in particular you don't want to get wet, just in case we do get a couple of feet of water?"

"What kind of trouble are they supposed to be having?"

"I hear rumors of everything from a crack in the face of the dam to the whole thing completely collapsing. I'm having a hard time getting too worked up about it. I'm afraid. I'm a little put out at having to leave my work."

Again I felt a surge of anger that this unfounded hearsay had not only messed up my day, but now was playing havoc with Conn's as well.

"Now honey, listen carefully. This could well be just a rumor, but I don't want you to take the slightest chance, if there is even a remote possibility that it is true."

He continued. "If you can, get some of the records and files out of the office and carry them upstairs where they won't get damaged by the water. But Clare, don't take a chance of any kind! Get out as quickly as you can. I'll leave here right away and get home as soon as I can make it."

His voice was strong and gentle and radiated his concern. He was quiet for just a second, and then he said, "Hey, sweetie, I love you."

And the wire went dead. I hung up the phone and with a hurried good-bye to Nicki I dashed back to the car.

As I started to back away, two men from St. Anthony drove up, and I paused to ask them if they knew any facts at all. Their only reply was that the sheriff had asked for volunteers to come out and make sure the area was completely evacuated. "Do you need any help?" was their next question.

"You bet your life!" I answered, and they followed me

70

back up the lane to the house. We ran to Conn's basement office and started to carry up the heavy file drawers to safety in the kitchen. The water was now less than thiry minutes from the house, but there was no sign of the coming destruction. The day was as quiet and beautiful as ever.

For a long time after the flood, I wondered why both Conn and Jon had a far greater premonition of danger when they heard of the dam failure than I seemed capable of feeling. The main reason was, I realized in retrospect, that as the two of them had watched the construction of the mammoth structure in the canyon above us they had personalized the situation, recognizing the tremendous capacity for destruction that was there if the dam should ever break.

5

Crisis!

My seventh trip up the steep, winding basement stairs was interrupted by the sound of the kitchen door being slammed shut. "Mom!" It was Jon's voice, edged with panic. "Where are you?"

"I had to get some of this stuff out of the basement, honey. Why on earth did you come back here?" I was honestly puzzled.

"Mom, I had to come back and get you out of here!" His voice was higher in pitch than it normally was, but he had regained some of the color in his face.

At that moment one of the men from town ran into the house. Everyone is in such a hurry, I thought. They are going to feel so silly when this is all over and they see there was no reason to hurry so fast. "Shall we try to get some of the machinery out?" his question came, but it was more of a statement than a request for information.

The machinery! The tractors, trucks, combines, and the other equipment to get the crop in and harvested. Some farmer's wife I had turned out to be!

"Oh, of course, we'd better try to get it somewhere where it won't get wet," I said, probably a trifle too fast. I was embarrassed that I hadn't thought fast enough to make the suggestion first. I turned to Jon.

"You drive the little Ford tractor out, Jon, up to the corner, and I'll follow you in the big white truck."

Bob Bauer, the man who made the suggestion, is a

distant cousin of Conn's and had grown up on a nearby farm. He nodded in agreement. "That should be plenty far. The water has never even touched this house, but you may have to come in and out for the next several days in a boat. The road is by far the lowest part of the place."

Jon ran out to get the small tractor started. He had been driving it all spring as he helped Conn with the different farming operations. Recently it had been used for spraying and it still had the spray rig attached to it. He jumped on the machine, started the motor, and drove out of the yard. He was driving way too fast again, I thought. And then, disgusted with myself, I mumbled, "I am really obsessed with his speed and safety today."

Walking out to the storage shed where the trucks were kept, I looked at the big white one with some trepidation. I had not used a manual gearshift in years, but boldly I climbed up into the huge conveyor truck, pushed in the clutch, and stepped on the starter. The huge engine roared to life with a bellow that nearly unstrung me. Taking a deep breath, I shifted the gear, stepped on the accelerator, and the truck leaped backwards, nearly killing my two volunteers from town. "Chalk up one for the monster," I muttered to myself as the men leaped for their lives. I tried to muster a feeble grin and jammed the gear shift into another position. Slowly the truck lurched out of the yard like a rheumatic dinosaur and I thought hotly, "This stupid rumor is going to get someone killed yet!"

The road beyond our lane had just been covered the day before with six inches of sand and gravel, as the county was preparing to oil it after years of neglect. The tires of the truck wavered as I turned the beast onto the road.

"My, that is really slippery!" I remember thinking,

and suddenly, with horror, I looked ahead of me at Jon driving the tractor.

He had never driven in loose gravel before, and now, in his overwhelming fear, he was going far too fast. I watched in shock as the tractor began to skid, and I knew, as surely as I had ever known anything in my life and with a terrible gnaw of fear and nausea building inside me, that he was completely out of control and had no hope of getting it back.

The tractor is going to roll on him. He is going to die in less than a minute, and it is all so unnecessary. He will be crushed to death and then we will find out that there was no need to heed this lie that has everyone scared to death! And I will be responsible for killing Jon, because I told him to drive that devilish machine down to the corner and I knew there was no need when I gave him the order. I just lost my head and panicked like everyone else in this foolish nightmare!

The words, one at a time, burned themselves into my mind as I watched the slow-motion nightmare—the long, deliberate sideways skid of the tractor, the frantic over-correction as Jon desperately fought his terrifying predicament, and the petrifying dance of death as the tractor began to roll slowly over. Jon's face, which was so plain and clear for me to see, was a mask of terror. I knew he was completely aware of what was about to happen to him and, like the other incredible events of this unbelievable day, was completely out of his power to change.

"Oh, God!" I screamed, above the roar of the tractor. "Don't let him die!"

The right wheel of the tractor began to raise off the ground as it started into its lethal roll.

My mind flashed back eleven years to the day our doctor friend Fran, Conn's fishing and hunting partner in San Jose, phoned us just as we were leaving the house for a long weekend in the redwoods of northern California. In his strong, booming voice Fran said, "Congratulations! Your son has just arrived!" The boy we had both decided we must adopt to complete our family of beautiful daughters had just been born that September day.

He was bright and handsome and lovable, and all our friends said he would have to become the most spoiled child in the universe. My answer was always the same. "We have no intention of spoiling him in any way. We simply treat him as we would any other three-day-old genius who happened to join our family!"

His gentle, quiet spirit was so like Conn's, and his complexion and eyes and smile so like mine that few people were aware he was adopted until we told them. He had always been everything we had hoped for in a son, and now I was going to lose him before I had ever really had time to know him as a young man. The tears streamed down my face as I pleaded with God to let him live.

The tractor stood as if suspended between the earth and sky for what seemed forever. Through my tears I watched in agony for it to complete its revolution, crushing Jon underneath. An eternity seemed to pass, and then I knew that the slender spray pipe that extended six feet beyond the tractor on either side was holding the tractor upright. It tore into the ground, gradually bending with the weight of the machine, but holding long enough for the tractor to be pushed back onto its wheel by its own momentum. In seconds, Jon shakily brought the machine to a stop.

I stopped the truck and raced for Jon. As if his joints were made of water, he staggered off the tractor and fell into my arms. White-faced, Bob Bauer, who had been following us, drove both pieces of equipment into the neighboring yard, while Jon and I stood in the road, trembling and in deep shock.

76

Bob drove us back to the house and Jon sat down in my car while I went back into the house for one last quick look around. Everything was so dear and familiar and warm and quiet. The stillness was shattered by the ring of the telephone, and Nancy's voice came shrilly over the wire.

"Mother, what are you doing out there? Get out! Get out right this minute. Hurry! You don't have any time left! You are going to be killed if you stay there any longer!"

"Now, Nancy, don't worry. I'm on my way. I just had to take care of a few things here. I'll be there in just a few minutes. Just wait for us."

"Mom! Hurry!"

I replaced the receiver and walked out of the house. The day was still warm and sunny. The men were still trying to secure the last of the machinery, quietly marveling at my calmness, which was not calmness at all but a deep shock that would not wear off for at least three days. My mind was still completely absorbed with the horror of seeing Jon nearly die, and I had become numb with the occurrences of this whole incredible day. I was consumed by anger and denial. It was not that I did not think this *could* happen to this particular Christian. In the heat of the events that were going on, I didn't even think about fairness or lack of it. I was simply stunned to the point of functioning totally on instinct.

I have never been sure whether anyone, family included, recognized what was going on in my life. Like nearly everyone who knew me, those close to me believed my faith in Christ was so strong that there was no question that I would be triumphant over tragedy. That was certainly true in the long run, but for the first few days I needed someone who was mature in Christ who would do several things for both Conn and me. We did not need Romans 8:28 quoted to us several times a day.

What we desperately needed in those first hours was someone who would hold us very tightly and remind us of two things. First, that God was definitely in control, and He had never let go for even a small minute. (We knew that mentally, but oh how we needed someone who could remind us of that over and over again, until we finally really *heard* it!)

And second, there never was a time in our lives when we more urgently required someone to tell us that things would not always be as they were in the first three days after the flood. For the first seventy hours after the flooding, which would prove to be such a critical time, I needed the perspective of someone who had loved me and laughed with me and shared the good things with me to stand by me and tenderly, constantly remind me of how God had worked in the past and how He would surely work again.

Things would have been different in that way, I am sure, had the telephone communications not been completely destroyed. Joyce Landorf, one of my dearest and most mature Christian friends, was trying frantically to get through to us. When she finally did, after three days, her blessed, alive voice communicated the healing warmth of love and caring I had needed so terribly in those first hours. She knew as she talked to me how deeply in shock I was, and for the life of me I can't remember anything more about our conversation than the enormous lift I got from knowing she *cared*. Joyce and I had laughed together and cried together often; she was the one person I needed at that moment more than anyone else. God provided her for me.

Conn's old friend Bufe Karaker called a few minutes later, and both those calls changed many things for us. Many well-meaning Christians could reply that I had the Holy Spirit to remind me of my source of strength and power in Christ, and I would surely admit they are certainly correct. But I have found many times in my Christian walk that there are times when we need someone with a face and an audible voice, and I believe without a doubt that is why God gives us Christian family and friends.

We were going to need that family more than ever in the next few weeks.

6

When Dams Collapse

After the water broke from the dam at 11:57 A.M., it moved down the narrow canyon in an incredible torrent one hundred feet high. A roar like that of freight trains pierced the quiet of the day as the imprisoned river broke angrily through the confining wall that had been the Teton Dam. Men from the Bureau of Reclamation and Morris-Knudson, the prime contractors, had been fighting since early morning what many of them were realizing was a losing battle—to save the giant structure from collapse. Along with a few tourists watching from the visitor's viewpoint and a couple of curious reporters who had heard there were some problems at the site, they watched in hypnotized horror as the multimillion-dollar pile of dirt and concrete fought a slow-motion tumbling act, and suddenly, with a resounding boom, was gone. The battle was over; the valley had lost.

Brawny construction workers, who had always taken enormous pride in the tough, competent job they handled for their organization, fought back the first tears many of them had experienced in a long, long time. Racing for their cars and trucks, they dashed down the narrow two-lane farm-to-market highway, hoping against hope that they could still get their families and loved ones out of the way of the devastating Teton River.

As the water raced from the canyon it split into five fingers of water. People fishing in the canyon below the dam were unaware of any problem until, without warning, clear water became muddy, rolling water rising suddenly with alarming speed and fury. Some rowed frantically for shore, where they were dumped unceremoniously fifty feet higher than where they had entered the water that morning. The others were swept downstream to serious injury or death.

The river marched along on its deadly course, spreading out over the valley in a massive force of destruction. As the water moved on it picked up more and more power. The very homes, farm buildings, and equipment that were destroyed became in turn devastators themselves, as they added their weight and bulk to that of the water itself.

On it moved across the valley, spreading like a great brown pestilence, tearing trees from their roots and houses from their foundations. The contents of homes, the countless possessions that are a million memories, were never to be seen again. They were gone, as if they had never been at all.

As the tidal wave of ruin moved across the valley floor, a great cloud of dust began to move before it. This cloud was perfectly visible for miles; I could easily have seen it from the farm had I looked to the east unstead of to the south where the river bed was, and from where I assumed the water *must* come. As I came out of the house for the last time, the water was less than a mile away and was moving toward us at a steady six miles per hour. But I never saw it. I was looking in the wrong direction.

I walked out of the house, my eyes glued to the south, searching for some sign that the dam had indeed broken and that the river was really rising. The sight in that direction was the same pastoral scene that had always been there. The two horses grazed quietly in the pasture, and far beyond them I could see the tall trees and clumps of willows that had lined the river undisturbed for nearly a hundred years.

I walked slowly down the sidewalk and paused at the stone gateposts that guarded the entrance to the yard. The men, waiting for me in the yard, were looking to the northeast, watching with horror as the advancing dust cloud bore down on the farm. I was in no hurry at all. Quietly, gently, protective of women to a fault, the men did not want to frighten or alarm me more than was absolutely necessary. I wondered aloud if the horses would be all right. The men said emphatically that they could look out for themselves. The flood was now less than three minutes from the farm, and horses were rapidly becoming the last thing the men were worried about!

Still in shock, I got into my car. Jon, white-faced and tense, sat completely silent beside me. Irish Red, the setter and family pet, who sensed somehow in her animal way that things were very wrong, curled up in a tight ball in the back seat. Very carefully, not about to court another skid on the loose gravel, I started down the road to town.

As we approached the first crossroad I looked over at Jon. Tears were streaming down his face, unchecked and apparently unheeded. "Mom," he said softly, and with a terrible sadness in his young voice, "is it really true that *everything* works together for good to those who love God?"

From his voice and the way he phrased the question, I got the impression that he had some real doubts about the answer. I knew his question was valid. He needed an honest answer. He deserved one. Actually, the same question had crossed my mind.

"Well, honey, that's what the Bible says, doesn't it? And since it doesn't say 'everything but a flood' I think we can assume that this will work for our good, too.'' My answer was probably not the most theological in the world, and it was a little slow in coming, but it was the best I could do for both of us right then.

Now the tears were really flowing, and Jon's next words were very choked.

"If it's true [and I got the distinct impression he had some very real reservations], then why am I so afraid? I'm a Christian!''

Oh, nuts! I thought. Why doesn't anyone ever ask me such profound questions when I have just come from a great Bible study or conference and I have some profound answers? So far, in ten years nobody ever had. They always managed to come up with them in a moment like this, when I was confused or tired or hurting and had no answers for myself, let alone someone else.

But he had to be answered. So I took a deep breath, silently asking God to provide me with a lot of wisdom in a great big hurry since I had none at all in that moment, reached over to touch Jon gently on his arm, and opened my mouth for some kind of answer.

"Well, Jon, I guess there are a couple of good reasons for that,'' I started. He seemed in that moment too young and vulnerable to be asking such tough questions. I had never loved him more.

"In the first place, you are honest. Lots of people get the idea—the wrong idea, but still they get it—that Christians are never scared or confused. That's just plain not true. Most of us are, at least once in a while, but for some reason we hate to admit it for fear people will think we are not Christians at all, or at least pretty shaky ones!

"And in the second place, God never promised for a minute that we'd like everything that happened to us, or even that we would understand it at the time. After all, even Jesus said, 'Father, why have you forsaken me?' And if He could ask I guess it's all right for us to ask, too.

84

But God has given us a promise, and His Word is always good, Jon. In the end, things that happen will work together for our good and for His glory."

Jon sighed a long sigh and we were quiet for a minute. That answer was to come back to me again and again in the next few weeks, during the tough and confusing moments in my own life when I doubted that even God could make sense of this mess that had suddenly invaded our lives. But Jon was satisfied for the moment, at least. His tears slowly stopped and he gave me an answering pat on the arm and a small, slow smile.

"Let's just pray, honey, and ask God to protect the farm and Dad as he comes home, okay?"

"Good idea." Jon waited until I had started to pray before he bowed his head and closed his weary eyes. I gathered he wanted to make sure one of us was still watching the road. He has a powerful sense of self-preservation, and he had had enough close calls for one day! Together we asked God's protection for the farm, especially for the house, since I knew how much Conn loved it, and for Conn himself as he hurried home.

We drove the rest of the way into town without conversation. As we neared the main highway I was surprised by the number of cars and trucks on the road. For the first time since we had left San Jose I was in a traffic jam! I felt like I had entered civilization again.

The traffic moved into St. Anthony at a snail's pace and the streets were crowded with people and cars. The scene had a nightmare quality about it—in spite of all the congestion no one was saying a word. The only sound was the blare of the local radio station, which must have been turned on in every car, giving matter-of-fact reports of the progress and damage the rampaging river was making. The faces of the people on the street mirrored shock and disbelief, and I saw I was not alone in my inability to comprehend the disaster. The biggest concern I had for the moment was where on earth I could find Nancy in all that mass confusion.

I followed cars around the corner, remembering then why I hated traffic jams—you have to go with the traffic in your lane. Too late I realized I should have been in the outer lane. As I turned the corner, disgusted with my inattentive driving, I nearly ran down a little red Karmann Ghia—its owner as obviously unaccustomed to this sudden traffic as I. There was only one Ghia in St. Anthony, and its annoyed driver, trying to get out of the way of my larger car, was none other than Nancy herself!

Oblivious to everything else for a moment, we both jumped out of our cars and hugged each other. Traffic stopped around us; everyone seemed to understand. Nancy was sobbing; she had been sure Jon and I had been caught in the water and drowned.

When I had not seemed the least bit alarmed or hurried by her phone call, which had come in the last minutes before I left the farm, she had decided to come back and help us. Overwhelmed with guilt that she had left without helping me get things out, she made up her mind to drive back out to the farm.

She had come through one roadblock on her way into town, so at first she assumed there was no way to get back in that direction. But then she remembered a second, less traveled route. A smaller farm-to-market blacktop road led out toward the farm, a half-mile further east of the main highway. Closer to the dam and a little longer way to the farm, Nancy headed for the old road, confident she could slip through in time to reach the farm and hurry me along.

Moments before she arrived at the edge of town, hastily appointed sheriff's deputies drafted from the local townspeople had also remembered the old road. They raced to the edge of town and set up temporary bar-

ricades. As Nancy approached her heart sank. She
realized she was too late to get through. Her voice breaking, she rolled down the window of the car and tried her
best to talk her way through the barrier. But it was no
use. The deputies would not allow her to drive into the
flood zone.

Minutes before Nancy had come, a pickup truck carrying three young men had rolled down the same highway,
intent on helping relatives get their possessions out of the
way of the water. As they left town, none of them could
possibly have known that they had less than five minutes
to live. Racing toward the Wilford area to help their
families pack up and get out, their pickup was engulfed
by the giant wave and they were all swept away to their
deaths. Had Nancy thought of the old road even five
minutes sooner than she did, she too would have died.

Together we went to a friend's house to wait for Conn
to come home. The hours began to drag on and there was
no word from him. Others who had been at the conference with him arrived home and reported in some surprise that he had left before anyone else. Then there
would be a sudden, awkward silence, as if they had
somehow said too much. It began to dawn on me that he
should have been home long ago. For the second time in
less than four hours, I felt the icy grip of fear—that Conn
had somehow gone through all the roadblocks in a futile
effort to reach the farm, and the Teton River had forever
torn him from us.

After talking with me early that afternoon, Conn had
hung up the telephone and stepped from the noisy dining
room at the retreat center into the clear mountain air.
The sun was shining warm and brightly as it had throughout the morning. Yet suddenly the warmth was gone.
Conn felt the dark edges of fear moving into his life.
Because of his size and strength he was a stranger to

87

panic, but in the wake of one short telephone message he was suddenly very afraid. His hands were clammy as he reached the room where the meetings were being held and quickly told the leader about the call he had just received.

Conn and I had known each other for over thirty years, and he knew I could handle emergencies when I had to. He also knew I could panic easily over a mouse in the bathroom or a child who did not return home at the assigned hour. He had a terribly uneasy feeling about the dilemma now. He had seen the dam; he had watched its construction and as a builder, he knew its terrible potential for disaster in the valley if the story were really true about its collapse. He wished with all his heart he could be at the farm right this minute. Instead, he was fifty miles and at least that many minutes away from home.

Picking up the few things he had brought along for the overnight stay, Conn walked quickly to his truck and was the first one out of the parking lot and down the winding mountain road. Perhaps it *was* only a rumor that had gotten out of hand. "Please, God, let it be that," he prayed silently as thoughts raced through his mind. Reaching over to turn on the radio, hoping against hope to hear nothing but the usual noon news and music, he raced the truck down the hill. His heart sank as he heard the report that was coming over the air. According to eyewitnesses, the reporter was saying, the Teton Dam had given way completely.

He soon reached the main highway and drove as fast toward the farm as he dared. Within minutes he had come to the point of the first roadblock. He had expected there would be roadblocks, but not so soon. He slowed, rolling down his window as the pickup came to a halt. A nervous patrolman, tension showing in his face, stepped to the window.

"I'm sorry, sir. This is as far as I can let you go on this

road. The highway is closed ahead due to the dam collapse.''

The words were spoken in a wooden manner, almost as if the man were reading a script, and a little apologetically, as though he hated to inconvenience travelers by a dam failure. Conn scarcely heard the words, replying quietly, "I'm sorry, too, but I am going on through. My family is down there and I have to do what I can to make sure they are safely out.''

His words were as softly spoken as the officer's had been, but there was no questioning the fact that Conn intended to back up each one of them, no matter how he had to do it. The officer hesitated for a moment and then stepped back.

"Then go ahead, sir, and the best of luck."

The last words were not yet out of his mouth as Conn put the Blazer in gear and raced on past the barricade. In less than thirty minutes he had reached the brow of the hill overlooking the valley. He took a deep, heartsick breath as he saw the great brown lake forming in the valley as the dam water moved steadily over the lush farmland.

The only thought that now consumed him was whether he could beat the water as it drove its slow but relentless path of destruction toward the farm. Then he realized there was a second, and apparently even more determined guard in the road just ahead of him. He halted the Blazer once more, and a heavy-set sheriff's deputy stepped up to the window.

"This is as far as you go, mister. I have orders not to let *anyone* past this point."

The man was big and burly and tough and young. And very frightened. He lived in that valley, and had been riveted with alarm as he watched the flood steadily filling the basin below. There was no way for anyone to prevail over the savagery of that water any more. And yet his heart ached for the people who were desperate to find out where their families were and if they had reached safety in time.

"I'm sorry," Conn repeated for the second time in less than an hour. "I am going through. My family is down there and I have to try to get them out." His words were spoken as firmly as the deputy had delivered his ultimatum.

"No way, mister! Those are my orders. Nobody goes through this block. You'd just die down there, mister. I am not letting you through!"

Conn put the Blazer in gear. Stonily, he met the other's eyes, and then he spoke. "Move back, son. You've done your duty and you've warned me, but I am going through on this road. I will either go past you or, if you prefer, I will drive over you, but I am going past! Take your choice."

With the truck moving toward him, the deputy decided Conn definitely meant what he said. With a sigh, he stepped clear of the road. Conn saw a look of frustration come over the young man's face as he drove past, as if he were wondering whether God took care of such idiots or whether perhaps this was how He eased them out of the world. The guard watched the red Blazer as it moved through the block. That would be the last vehicle through on this road for many months to come.

The race was against time now. The water appeared to be moving very slowly, but it had a force Conn never dreamed of. He drove into the little town of Teton City, just a mile east of the farm, and slowed as he saw two brothers he had known as a child.

"Just saw your barn floating away, Conn."

In any other setting the words would have been remarkably bizarre. But now Conn simply stared, almost unable to comprehend what he was hearing.

"Are you sure it was my place, Vern?" he asked,

remembering how as small boys he and Vern had played for hours in the hayloft of the huge red barn.

" 'Fraid so, Conn." Vern's voice was slow and sad. " 'Fraid so."

Conn drove away. He slowed as he neared the turn onto Pole Line Road, which runs north and south along the boundary of the farm. What he saw from the highway convinced him he could not possibly turn onto the road. He watched, fascinated, as the water swept a newly built home from its foundations, realizing that that was exactly the way Vern had seen the barn go. Conn glanced in the rear-view mirror and saw that he had just seconds to get out of the way of the second rush of water that was coming at the Blazer from the south as well as from the northeast! With a quick prayer for me, Jon, and Nancy, he moved on down the road toward Rexburg, where Julie and Carl and their two little girls, Amanda and Rebecca, lived.

Within minutes he was at the small subdivision on the north side of Rexburg. Julie and Carl had lived there just a few months and were finally getting settled and beginning to see progress on their lawn and yard. The new subdivision was still so new that most of the families who lived there were just starting to prepare their yards for planting.

The housing development was less than one hundred fifty yards from the river. Word had been received more than an hour earlier that residents would have to evacuate their homes. Like so many others who heard the news that morning, Carl and Julie had some trouble believing the dam had actually broken. Carl's first impulse, on hearing of trouble, had been to come up to the farm and help sandbag the river.

A friend, Marie Douglass, called Carl from St. Anthony and told him—in no uncertain terms—that he had to get Julie and the girls out of danger immediately, and because of her urgency Carl listened. As the reports kept coming over the radio, he became convinced very quickly that this was not a sandbagging operation! Julie had been very ill for the past several months with a back injury, and Carl was reluctant to move her from their home. Yet he knew he had no choice.

Taking a few changes of clothing for the children and diapers for the baby, they started out of the house. For several years Carl had been a professional photographer for Campus Crusade for Christ. He had kept an unusually good photographic record of their marriage and of our family as well. Julie hesitated as she passed the shelves that held the slides. They were in several large boxes and it would be such an easy matter to grab them on the way past and throw them in the trunk of the car. Probably no need, she decided. They were well up on the shelves, and surely the water would not get high enough to do them any damage. They left the house, locked the door, and drove to a friend's house who lived high on one of the hills on which Rexburg is built.

After making sure that Julie and the girls were safe and comfortable, Carl drove back to their house to make sure his neighbors were all safely out. Gradually, even the stragglers were convinced that the danger was real, and Carl was getting into his car for the last time as Conn drove up.

"Are you all okay, Carl?"

Conn's first words mirrored the concern Carl was feeling for our family.

"They're fine. I just took them up to Webster's to stay until the water goes down and we can come back to the house. How about Mom and Jon and Nancy?"

Conn just shook his head. "I don't know. I wish I did."

Police cars filed through the neighborhood, urging those remaining to hurry to higher ground. Conn followed Carl up the winding streets to the home of our friends, Jane and Bill Webster. Everyone stood outside, watching as if hypnotized as the great swirl of brown water advanced on the north part of the city. No one spoke. Julie finally broke the silence. She was sitting down and could not see as well as the others.

"Carl," she asked, "can you still see our house?"

It was their first home. They had scrimped and saved for the down payment and then furnished it with more imagination and love than money. It had been a warm and comfortable house for them, filled with happy memories.

"No," answered Carl, but with what he hoped was a voice of reassurance he said, "but I can see the trees from here."

With a sinking heart but an ever-practical mind, Julie responded, "Oh, Carl, there aren't any trees in our neighborhood!"

She was right. The trees Carl could see from the hill had been growing just below the dam!

Seeing that Carl and Julie were at least temporarily settled and comfortable, Conn started on the long, circuitous route around the valley to get home. It was nearly 150 miles for a trip that should have taken ten minutes could he have used the same road home he had driven down on, but now he had to travel around the destruction and go above the dam. As he drove, he prayed.

"Lord, you know that the most important thing for me right now is that Clare and the kids are safe. She sure didn't sound like she knew how bad this was on the phone this morning, and now I need you to keep them safe."

Immediately, as if in answer to his prayer, Conn knew we were all right no matter what may have happened. With an overwhelming sense of peace, he remembered he had prayed for us that morning as he awakened, and he had a real assurance that God had answered that prayer and was indeed tenderly and watchfully caring for all three of us.

As he drove along, Conn remembered for some reason that it was the fifth of June, almost ten years to the day since I had come home from a meeting nearly bursting with news I could not keep to myself. It had been a long, hot day in San Jose, California, in 1966. For years we had been religious and frustrated, and then I brought home the news that there was a way to know God personally. I had asked Conn to come back to the meeting with me that night so he could share in my joyful discovery.

The speaker, a businessman like Conn, had talked that afternoon about asking Jesus to come into your life. According to him, He would come and you could know God in a personal way. I had been preparing for that news for months in Nell's Bible study, but Conn had not and he was not only less than eager, he was not even slightly interested.

I thought somehow I must have explained the whole thing to Conn wrong, and was more convinced than ever that if only he would go with me so he could hear the message in the right way, he would be eager to ask Christ into his life, too.

Evangelism—Conn hated that word! It sounded to him like some ranting, raving preacher with a cheap suit and a southern accent shouting at him to be "saved," whatever that was supposed to mean. He found it totally repulsive and completely out of step with his world.

Conn was a self-made man and mighty proud of it. He had built a million-dollar business from a shovel handle, and he had done it nearly single-handedly. He was greatly respected in the construction community as an honest builder whose word was as good as his bond, and whose work could always be trusted to be of the very highest quality. He was a man's man—a man who loved to hunt and fish and could drink with the best of them, but who never became obnoxious in the process. Conn was proud that he was not one of those goody-goody characters he had come to associate with church and missionary work.

Oh, he did go to church. Religiously. He would hastily tell you that he was as good as anyone else he knew—in the church or out of it. He was always willing to serve on the building committees, and he usually did. He gave freely of both his time and his money to the church. He even gave a tenth of his income, albeit a bit grudgingly at times. Wasn't that enough, for heaven's sake? Conn often said that the trouble with the world is that there are too many who are talking religion and not enough who are willing to live the Golden Rule.

He thought I had been acting just a little bit funny for a long time now, especially since I'd started attending Nell's Bible class. What on earth did I want from him now? he thought. He would let me go to my evangelism meetings if they made me happy. Maybe I needed them. Conn knew he did not.

Of course, my life had been changed that day. When I came home from the afternoon meeting I had the peace and joy I had seen for so long in Nell, and it was a heady experience. I felt like I had come back to a warm, welcoming home after a very long, cold journey, and how I wanted Conn and the children to share it with me!

As Conn looked at me in the early evening that June day, he was disturbed. He liked our lives the way they were; he didn't want me to rock the boat, and he sensed that that was very definitely happening. In the years of our early marriage in Idaho, and then later during our years in business in California, he had been the initiator and the pacesetter in our marriage. He was instinctively afraid of anything he could not completely control. The simplest way he could see to get us back on the track—his track, that is—was to go to the "blasted meeting" with me and show me the error of my ways. Somehow these fanatics had gotten a hold on me and were about to lead me astray, and there was no way Conn Bauer would let that happen right in front of his eyes. And so that night Conn went to the meeting with me.

The meeting wasn't anything like he had thought it would be. Nobody was barking at the moon or throwing sawdust in the air. The businessman speaker was soft-spoken and obviously, worse luck, as successful as Conn himself. Reluctantly, grudgingly, Conn found himself listening to the man's words.

There were four things Howard Ball said that night. Everyone, according to him, needed to know them. The first was that God loves us and has a wonderful plan for our lives.

"Whoopeedoo!" thought Conn. "So what's new? I love me and I have a wonderful plan for my life, and I really haven't done too badly at putting it in motion. I really doubt that God has a better one for me than I do. I'll have to remember to tell Clare this when we get home, so she won't get too carried away by this nonsense."

Howard's second point was that man is sinful and thus separated from God. Therefore, he cannot know or experience God's love and forgiveness and His plan for one's life.

"Oh, so what?" said Conn to himself. "I haven't done anything too bad in my life. I haven't killed anyone, although I think a lesser man may have if he had been provoked as much as I have. I haven't committed adultery or anything like that—so far. I haven't stolen anything bigger than I could carry. So what's so sinful about my life?" Offhand, Conn thought, he could give you a list of at least thirty men who were a lot worse than he was, and some of them were very good church members! How about that, God?

"Jesus Christ," Howard continued, "is God's only provision for man's sin. Through Him you can know and experience God's love and plan for your life."

"The same old thing. They always have to come back to that, don't they?" Conn's thoughts raced ahead of the speaker. "Wasn't it enough just to go to church, do the best you can, and hope God will understand and give you the benefit of the doubt when the time comes for a final accounting?"

"But the fourth law is the key to the Christian life," the voice from the platform relentlessly continued. "You must receive Jesus Christ as your personal Savior and Lord. God doesn't have any grandchildren, you know. You have to ask Him to come into your life."

"There's the long slow curve, with the fast ball right behind it," thought Conn. "Fine. You give your life to God and the next thing you know, He tests you to see if you are serious, and just how much you can take. So He sends you off to Africa to be a missionary among the headhunters and the pygmies! None of that old stuff for me. If what I'm doing isn't good enough for God, that's just too bad. And if I'm not good enough for Clare, that's her tough luck!"

With that angry thought, Conn walked out of the meeting and sat in the car for the next hour and a half, waiting for me to finish. It was a very silent ride home.

I had seen Conn walk out, of course, and I knew he was thoroughly angry. I fully expected him to jump all over me, but instead I was greeted with an icy silence. When I finally got the courage to ask Conn what he thought of the speaker and his message, he muttered something about how they are all exactly alike with the same predictable message, and said not another word. That stony silence, broken very rarely, was to continue for six long months.

As Julie, Beck, and Lisa watched my life change, they were all puzzled at first, then relieved, and finally completely captivated by this Christ who could change an angry, uptight, insecure mother into a person they could genuinely enjoy and admire. And they became Christians, too. Conn was the one lonely, angry holdout. Wanting the peace and contentment he was seeing the rest of us enjoy, yet terribly afraid that the price God would ask of him would be far too high to pay, Conn became more and more withdrawn and resentful of the rest of the family.

And then finally, in the last week of December, the battle came to an end. Like so many skirmishes, the final attack came from a quarter none of us expected at all. Building had been at an all-time high for much of the year of 1966. After years of being in the construction business, we were enjoying our best year. But late in the fall the picture drastically changed almost overnight, it seemed. Interest rates began to skyrocket, and money to use for new building projects was suddenly dried up. Three large builders who each owed Conn large sums of money all declared bankruptcy, and Conn found himself facing the sickening fact that he had nearly a third of a million dollars in accounts receivable that was apparently impossible to collect. The debtors—suppliers who had provided the materials for the jobs—wanted their money. In a matter of days, Conn was forced to realize that the plan he had worked out so carefully for his life, and the company that he had built with such pride, was on the brink of insolvency.

Physical death held no terror for this big man. Conn had faced that years ago and come to grips with it. But bankruptcy was a different ball game. His pride, his word, his whole world lay on the line. He was in no way prepared to forestall the inevitable crash. He raged against it for weeks, and finally on the night of December 20, as his world collapsed around him in little pieces, Conn knelt in the living room of the house he had built with such love and pride and asked Jesus to come into his life. "God, make me the man you want me to be, no strings attached—even if it means preaching to the pygmies!" was my husband's prayer.

When God finally succeeds in getting a person's attention, the chosen man or woman usually finds out in a hurry that God did not want his or her business or talent or ability at all; He only wanted to be that person's God. God didn't want Conn's business or his abilities, as great or as small as they were. What God wanted was Conn and his willingness to say to Him, "All right, Lord. I will be your man for the rest of my life, and I give you the total freedom to use my life in whatever way you choose to use it." And God began to do just that.

The business did not fail. God did not hand it to Conn on a silver platter, but He did allow him to salvage some of the assets from the builders who owed him money. God did cause the bank to give Conn more time, which they had adamantly refused to do for weeks, and slowly Bauer Concrete began to come out of the financial slump that had come so close to completely undoing it. It became stronger than ever as Conn learned from his mistakes in the past and began to build an even more secure future.

But there was a very definite difference beginning in 1967. Conn's business no longer ruled his life. God became the master, and through the years, as Conn's relationship to God deepened and grew, his priorities changed. The business became a means to an end, rather than an end in itself. Conn wanted more than anything else to be in the center of God's will, and profits from the business were given to missionaries and churches in order that the gospel message of Jesus and His love might be heard everywhere. When we realized what a difference He had made to our family and how very close we had come to missing out, we cared very much that others would have an opportunity to hear and decide for themselves.

For the next eight years, from 1967 to 1974, Conn used the time, materials, and money that God provided through his occupation to help Christian schools, orphanages, churches, and missionaries in other parts of the world. Our home was open to several Christ-centered organizations to be used in whatever way it could be used. Our world and that of our children became much wider and deeper and satisfying as others shared with us how God was using their lives for His kingdom. We watched with joy as Julie married Carl and they joined the staff of Campus Crusade. A few years later Beck married Larry, who worked with Youth for Christ.

By 1974, however, all of us knew there were changes in the air. Conn became more and more convinced that the time had come to leave California and move back to Idaho. We found that, with much prayer, God prepared us all well for the move. It was not an easy one for any of us, but because we believed it was where God wanted us, it made the whole thing much easier to take.

As he was making the long journey and recalling these past events, Conn believed with all his heart that he and his family lived on the farm because that is where God wanted us to be. And now, with the collapse of a federal dam, he found himself wondering if there would be anything left or if he would have to start all over again. There was no way for him to know if the farm had been totally destroyed; it seemed very likely. He wondered if he would have the strength to go on. But he did know beyond the shadow of a doubt that ten years before he had trusted a God who is infinitely faithful and loving. That, for the moment, would have to be enough.

7

Some Through the Waters

As Conn was making his long, winding drive back toward St. Anthony, the hours wore on for those of us who were waiting. Everyone was becoming more and more tense and quiet as no word came from my husband. I knew every hour that passed only increased the possibility that he indeed had been swept away by the river. Yet I could find no way to share what I was thinking with Jon and Nancy. They were as frightened and incapable of expressing their fears as I was. My mother-in-law said nothing, but fear was written all over her dear face. Her expression told me her feelings far better than any words could. Friends called periodically to see if there was any word, and when the reply was negative they changed the subject so quickly it was painful for us both. There was simply nothing to say.

Then finally, around six in the evening, the stillness was broken by yet another phone call. My aunt in Ashton, the small town about fifteen miles north of us, was on the other end of the line and she was crying. A tough old pioneer woman, her sobs made me think I was finally going to know something for sure—something terribly bad. Then I understood what she was saying: Conn was there at her home! Sure enough, his strong vibrant voice, heavy with emotion, spoke gently in my ear the reassuring words that he was okay. For another moment there was still nothing to say. But now there was no need.

Conn said he was on his way to us, that Julie and Carl and the girls were safe, and that he would be there in a few minutes. I hung up, and with my arms around Nancy and Jon, cried the first tears of many that were to come in the next few days—tears of anger, of frustration, of fear and of sheer exhaustion. But these first tears were of sheer, unadulterated joy.

Later in the evening we sat down to eat the dinner prepared by the loving hands of my mother-in-law. Conn had arrived and she asked him to say grace, and he said he could not pray right then. He asked me if I could, and I simply thanked God that we could still trust Him, even though it appeared to me that things were really in the biggest mess I had ever seen in my life.

I believe in honest prayer, and for the next few days I was going to pray some of the most honest prayers of my life. Most of the time I would be screaming at God about the whole predicament. I could not see the day and its events as a blessing; I knew I had to thank God in faith, and believe me, that is the only way I could thank Him. I could see absolutely no virtue in making or allowing a mess of this size or scope, and I believed God was responsible for it. The worst of it was that I knew, with a very sick feeling, that a lot of people were looking at us and saying, "Let's see how Christians accept this!" Or worse yet, "If they were really Christians, would God let this happen to them?" Not all of them, by any means, were sympathetic.

We decided to drive out to the farm and see how bad the damage really was. I still found it hard to believe it was more than a two- or three-foot water problem, even after Conn told me of his conversation with Vern Gould. Of course, there were many reports constantly coming over the radio and now on television, but I still doubted very much that the farm could possibly be as badly damaged as the reports seemed to indicate. I was still determined to believe that this was all just a rumor totally out of control. My mind simply could not take in all the reports of damage that others were now claiming to have seen with their own eyes. When Conn told me about the barn floating away, I laughed aloud. That was too far-fetched to be anything but hysterically funny. I wondered what on earth caused people to imagine such things.

This air of unreality persisted as we drove out toward the farm. Roadblocks were still in place, as they would be for weeks to come, and once again Conn had to announce with great determination that we were definitely going to go through before we were allowed to continue on our way. The birds were still singing, the leaves of the trees still rustled softly in the twilight breezes, and the soft late afternoon sun gave a rosy glow to the countryside as we took the familiar road to the farm.

"This is far too pretty a day for such an awful thing to have happened," Nancy's voice reflected my thoughts, and I wondered again if indeed the whole day had been nothing more than a bad dream. Maybe I would soon wake up. Just at that moment, the road ended abruptly at a four-mile-wide river!

There was no warning whatsoever. Where there had been farms and homes, lawns and trees and flowers, gardens and barns and livestock peacefully grazing, there was nothing but a river—a wide, muddy, rushing river that surged angrily on its way, determined, it seemed, that nothing should ever hold it back again.

For a long time there was complete silence in the car. It was almost as if everyone had stopped breathing. During that time, each of the four of us was utterly alone, locked in the shock and wonder of the reality that the worst had

105

indeed happened—that all the reports were true. The farm was really gone, along with a hundred others. Not a landmark was left for a reference point! Where do you even start looking for a two-hundred-acre plot of land when all you have to start with is a river as wide and as muddy as the Mississippi? But how can you possibly misplace a two-hundred-acre farm?

A hushed but excited voice from the back seat broke the stillness. Jon's sharp eyes had seen something!

"Look Dad, there's the house! I can see it. I think maybe it could be off the foundation, but it's still standing there!"

It was true. As we strained our eyes through the deepening twilight, we stared where Jon was pointing and saw the old log house, standing naked and unprotected in the middle of the water. Most of the trees around the yard were gone, those lovely trees that had given shade in the summer's heat and protection from the winter winds. The garage, whose door I had so carefully locked, the storage sheds, the huge barn—everything but the house had vanished and was no more. But the house still stood! Not knowing whether we should rejoice or cry some more we turned the car around and headed back toward town.

The night was long and sleepless for most of us. Jon was the only one who had no trouble; he fell asleep almost the moment his head touched the pillow. It is a fearsome thing to see a boy become a man in a single day. It is also exhausting, and Jon seemed somehow to sense that the days ahead would never again be the same carefree days he had known in summers past. And so, tired beyond belief, he slept. Sooner or later we all joined him in the welcome oblivion of sleep.

Sunday morning dawned cloudy and cool. There was no thought of church, which is so sad in retrospect.

There was never a moment when we needed that fellowship and love more. We decided, instead, to make the trip back out to the farm, this time with a borrowed rowboat, to see close up how bad the damage really was. Nancy chose not to go; she could not face the cold and the mud and the destruction so soon. And so the three of us—Conn, Jon, and I—drove down the familiar road once again, past the barricade—different guards, same protests—and parked about a mile from the house.

The water had receded somewhat during the night, and we were able to get much closer than we had the night before. We all got into the boat and rowed, without any conversation, across what had been a pasture filled with grazing cattle and a potato field. Finally we came to the tennis court north of the house, where we all got out of the boat and wordlessly plodded through the ankle-deep mud to the house itself.

I looked with stunned disbelief at the old house. That porch I had asked God to do something about had been taken care of. It would never leak on me or anyone else again because it had been torn away by the force of the water. That was the good news. The bad news was that the other porch—which had never leaked on anyone and held the steps to the house—was also gone! So were all the windows on the first floor. Instead of a wall on the south side of the dining room and kitchen, there was a great gaping hole.

I didn't dare look at the basement. I ruefully remembered my fears that I would have to clean up a mess down there. I was wrong about that. It wasn't a mess; it was a disaster. Filled with parts of trees and bushes, mud, small animals, and parts of machines and houses, it was completely filled to the top with the smelly, sickening remains of the tidal wave that ripped through. I didn't have to clean up a messy basement; it took a bulldozer and eight strong men to finally get all the muck out, after they had torn out one part of the cellar wall for a driveway for the dozer.

Conn helped me climb up over the remaining porch foundation. Together, without a word, we walked into our house, or what remained of it. Mud was three to four feet deep in every room on the first floor, and we both experienced a sickening feeling of loss as we realized that *everything* on that floor was gone. Disappeared. Vanished. It was as if some giant hand had brushed through each room and simply swept everything away. I had prepared myself to find things muddy and water-soaked and ruined, but I was completely unprepared for everything to have disappeared.

The refrigerator and the dishwasher had been washed out of the kitchen and through the wall, along with most of the cabinets and drawers. The dining room was completely bare except for the heavy chandelier that had apparently been free enough to swing above the water. It was filled with mud, but it was still there, hanging ghostlike and bedraggled above the empty room.

The living room was full of mud. The wallpaper, shredded and mud-stained, and one tattered drape moved forlornly with the breeze that swept through the room unhindered by window or door. The grand piano, Nancy's pride and joy, lay awkwardly in the south corner, crushed and crumpled with two of its three legs broken off. As I walked over to look at it closer my foot touched something unyielding in the soft mud. It was Nancy's flute, and it looked like it had gone through a sand-blasting machine. The mantle on the fireplace, so heavy that it had taken six men to lift it into place when the house was being built, was washed away.

A huge tree had rammed the house from the north; its trunk and remaining branches pushed into the living room and the little sitting room just to the left of it.

Beyond the sitting room the bathroom was filled with mud and more of the tree. Over the whole house was a terrible smell of filth and chemicals and mildew and death.

I looked at Conn, dazed by the evidence of the sheer destructive force that had come through this house. I dared not ask how bad he thought it all was. His face told me there was very little hope of salvaging the place, but even as I looked I knew he would move heaven and earth to save it.

Silently we walked up the stairs to the second floor. I had noticed as we came near the house in the boat that the upper windows were still intact. Yet every window on the lower floor, along with their sashes and in some cases part of their surrounding walls, was gone. The stairs turn sharply at a right angle near the top, and from that point on it was as if nothing had ever happened. The play room upstairs was as neat and clean as if it were just waiting for company. The bedrooms were fresh and tidy as I had left them that long-ago (it now seemed) Saturday morning. From up here it was such a normal world! Again I had the terrible disembodied feeling that this was a terrible nightmare.

We went together into our bedroom, where Conn sat down heavily on the bed. I walked into our closet to find an old pair of tennis shoes to wear for the clean-up work that I assumed would begin immediately. I found some that had been used for gardening and had definitely seen better days. As I came out of the closet with them, Conn looked at me and said the first words he had spoken since we started out in the boat.

"What are you doing with those shoes?"

I didn't understand his question. We had to start cleaning the mud out of the house. Surely he could see that. I answered him in a rather choked voice.

"I have to put on something that won't be ruined by the

mud. I thought we'd start digging out this morning. It's my house too, Connie.''

Tears and sobs began to rack his body. I didn't know what to do. I understood his hopelessness. A long time later, he told me he felt as if he had experienced a terrible death in the family. It was precisely that, of course. He had seen his dream die.

I stood beside him and held him in my arms. I was overcome with his despair and despondency. I was also very afraid. He was my rock and my strength. How could I possibly cope if he couldn't? And for a moment, I thought I was beyond tears and beyond hope. I knew I would never be strong enough to pull all this back together if he wasn't.

In the next few months I saw many women become bitter and angry as their husbands were unable to find the strength to start building again. I knew beyond a doubt what they were going through, and my heart ached for them. Their bitterness sprang from their inability to cope with their situation, and yet beyond that there was always the terrible feeling that if their husbands either could not or would not handle it, the women *had* to! And it was an impossible task.

I realized anew that God has ordained the husband to be the head of the home. If he refuses to take that position, or for some reason abdicates it, the wife is forced into the leadership in the marriage and the home. The result is disaster for everyone involved.

Without God and the freedom Conn had to completely admit his own weakness and helplessness, we too would have been in that spot. Because he had the freedom to cry, Conn was able to dry his tears and begin to honestly ask God for the wisdom and strength he knew he was lacking for the massive rebuilding job that lay ahead of us. Because I knew that my husband was depending on

God, I could trust his leadership and unhesitatingly follow him with a real joy and peace.

Our greatest need, humanly speaking, was to obtain enough manpower to help get the mud out of the house before the floors gave way under the terrific weight of the debris. We returned to town and began to do something that was very strange and very difficult for us.

During all of our Christian lives, and indeed, most of our adult lives, Conn had been on the giving end in any situation where help was needed. He had never had to ask anyone for assistance. Well, I want you to know, in case you don't already, that it is a thousand times easier to offer than it is to ask. The moment you must ask you have made yourself vulnerable—the one you ask may refuse to help.

For several weeks I failed to understand the apparent indifference of some whom we asked to help, until one day the pastor of the church came to call. As we talked he spoke in glowing terms of one of the neighbors. "You know, Clare, he was just remarkable through the whole thing, and so very strong!" His report simply radiated with praise. "When someone asked if they could help him, he answered that he didn't need any help. His place had just washed away and he had lost everything, but he was in great shape! He was asking everyone else what he could do to help them, even people who hadn't lost anything!"

I saw that man months later, and he was still unable to decide what to do to start rebuilding. But obviously, to the community at large and to our church in particular, it was considered a tremendous virtue *not* to appear weak enough to need help. The great "God helps those who help themselves" theory was again alive and well and thriving. Who wouldn't admire a man who could lose everything and seemingly not even bat an eyelash?

111

But I knew from our own lives that it was anything but a normal reaction. And yet the impression had been left that it was wrong to ask for help. The picture took a long time to come into focus for me until one day late in July when I stopped in Rexburg to see our young family doctor—not because I needed his professional help but because I was near his office and he was a good friend. He had been hurt by the flood, too; his home and office had been badly damaged.

As I sat in his office waiting for him to come in, I thanked God again that I was really healing from the trauma and could look back without bitterness. I knew I wasn't whole yet, but Conn and I were both well on the way, and I was grateful to God for that. Mark came in looking tired and harried, and when he saw me he sat down heavily in the other chair.

"Oh, boy, you really look great!" were his opening words, so spontaneous I knew they were completely sincere. "How do you do it anyway? I heard you and Conn were really wiped out the first week or so after this thing happened."

"Mark, honey, you really heard right!" I answered him with a smile. "But you know, Mark, God has very long arms, and He sent us friends from California and Texas and everyplace else to help us not only dig out, but to cry with us and hold us and give us the freedom to *be* devastated. Their love helped heal us."

He looked at me for a long moment and then said, slowly and thoughtfully, as if it were just occurring to him: "You know, Clare, it is the strangest thing. Those people who cried and fell apart in the first ten days are the ones who are starting to come back together again. But there are so many who didn't seem to have that freedom, and I want you to know I am seeing more people with breakdowns and mental collapse and attempted suicides than I ever dreamed I would in a lifetime of medical

112

practice. Isn't it funny? The strong ones are just not snapping back like you'd think they would."

How blessed it is to have the freedom in Christ to cry and feel broken when you suffer a loss! How wonderful to know that we don't have to be strong all the time, because we have a Savior who is.

We did ask for help, though, and God did send help from His people. From Los Gatos Christian Church and Northwest Baptist Church in California and from other places, they came, bringing money, supplies, and love. Some of those dear Christians came from over a thousand miles away, using vacation time they had saved all year for a much-needed rest for themselves and their families. Rest they would not get, but they would know the joy of helping a brother in his time of need. They came as the love of God impelled them to come, and not a single one came empty-handed. They brought sleeping bags and food, and cars and trucks and campers piled high with love gifts from others who could not come.

And Conn and I began to understand, in a brand new way, what the Christian community is all about. It does not mean merely belonging to the same church. It is people who are committed to Christ, yes, but they are also fully committed to their fellow Christians. It is impossible to be a real church without that. Through the next few months we received letters, money, gifts, and most of all *hope* as our fellow believers joined with us in a battle that had become their battle as well as ours.

Four days after the flood, Conn received a letter from an old friend, Weldon Hardenbrook. He had written the letter before he knew of the disaster, asking Conn to come with him to a meeting in Ohio to meet with Weldon's fellow elders and leaders in founding a new church. The meeting was to be held in early July. Conn read the letter, handed it to me, and asked what I thought about it. Frankly, the timing was so terrible I knew it had to come from God; no one else could possibly have had the audacity to ask Conn to leave at such a time!

In addition to the complete ruin we were facing over a long term, the river now stubbornly refused to go back into its old bed. All the efforts of the National Guard, and the Army Corps of Engineers, and the county commissioners had been completely useless. The river, once unleashed from the confines of the dam, seemed to have developed a mind of its own, and it was quickly becoming apparent that it was going to take a very special power to get the river back where it belonged. For nearly three weeks the battle continued. Many times as we went to bed in the mobile home Conn had moved to the farm, we did not know whether we would wake up in the morning on dry land or back in the river.

The deadline to sign up for the conference in Ohio drew closer, and Conn's final answer was that there was simply no way he could possibly leave the farm with the river still out of control. I felt so strongly that the summons to the meeting had come from God that, in a last-ditch effort, I asked Conn if he would pray with me that if God wanted him to go to the meeting He would put the river back in its place. I believe in taking your needs to God, and if a miracle is necessary it is up to Him to take care of it!

Conn and I prayed together, along with a close friend from San Jose who happened to call just as we were discussing it. I don't think for one minute that that friend, Pat Borgia, has a special hot line to heaven, but I do know she maintains close fellowship with God and is therefore on very good speaking terms with Him. Together we prayed, and two days later, early Saturday morning, when we looked toward the river, we saw that God had done what dozens of men and tons of equipment could not—the Teton was back in her bed, flowing along as smoothly as if she had never left it. On Sunday Conn

114

left for Ohio. That meeting was to change his life and the lives of all the rest of our family along with him. As a result of that meeting, a new church came into being in our area nearly a year later.

8

Some Through Anger, Confusion, and Tears

In my years as a Bible teacher I had studied and read about Satan and his tactics many times. For the first several days after the flood, however, I was to get a practical education in his ways that would forever enlarge and amplify my understanding in a way that all my reading and theories had not. There is a tendency among Christians, I believe, to give him more credit than he deserves. Sometimes our own human natures are causing our problems. But I think that more often than not—probably because we haven't been taught about Satan—we do fail to see him as the source of many temptations and trials.

In the first ten days after the flood I was engulfed in confusion and fear, neither one of which comes from God. Shock takes a terrible toll on any person, and as I watched Jon's near-miss accident and then feared for Conn I must have aged ten years. As we walked through the mud and debris of the flood's aftermath, I felt again an incredible confusion. How could God possibly have allowed this to happen to us? I began to blame Him for deserting us and leaving us without hope. We had given Him the farm as a gift, and now it lay a hopeless mess, ruined and devastated. Was that any way to treat a loving gift? I certainly didn't think so!

The first week ended. Lisa and Dave had come from California with their small son, Charlie. Beck and Larry flew in from Texas. I arranged housing for them, enormously grateful for their presence and their constant expressions of love. But in my terrible emotional exhaustion I could not tell them or anyone else how angry and betrayed I felt. After all, they were still my children and they had always looked to me for guidance and direction.

Fighting fear and depression and a monstrous growing anger, I could not see where in the world I could turn. Conn's problems both with the loss and with trying to decide where to start in the rebuilding were enough for him, I thought. Besides, I instinctively felt he had no answers right then either, and in expressing my feelings I would only add to his already intolerably heavy burden. The only place I could go was to God, and I was certainly not on my usual loving and joyful terms with Him! But He was the only one I could really rail at without fear of causing a nervous breakdown.

How I scolded Him and screamed at Him when I was alone in the car driving to and from the farm. I told Him how angry I was with Him and what a lousy manager I thought He was in taking care of the house and the farm. But no one else knew that. Besides being angry, you see, I was also very ashamed at what I considered a real lack of Christian maturity. I knew God loved me anyway, even while I was yelling at Him, but I wasn't at all sure it wouldn't make others stumble all over the place.

Over and over again we were reminded by well-meaning friends of how like Job we were in our circumstances. While I had never carefully studied Job, I did recall that his friends' advice was not exactly his greatest source of comfort in his trials, and I easily identified with that part of his story at least.

The climax to my angry confrontations with God came ten days after the flood, when Conn and I and three of the children—Nancy, Jon, and Beck—were all in the mobile home on the farm. Larry had gone back to Texas, Lisa and Dave were on their way home to California, and Julie and Carl were settled temporarily in a newly rented house in St. Anthony.

A ferocious wind storm came up. The wind blew harder and harder, and at one point its speed registered over sixty miles an hour. From inside the trailer it sounded like a hurricane!

The three children were in the back part of the mobile home playing a game, while Conn and I sat in the living room at the other end of the unit. For a while we tried to talk, but we soon gave that up as we found it nearly impossible to hear or be heard over the sound of the howling wind. I listened as the wind grew stronger and stronger outside, while inwardly I was silently raging at God. The tempest in my thinking was no less severe than that which was raging in the elements.

A letter had just come that day from a friend who said she knew we were going to be just like Job (that is, that God would replace everything—it was supposed to be comforting). I thought, "Gloria's probably right that we are just like Job. The next thing that is going to happen will be that this blasted wind is going to blow down one of the trees on the trailer and all three of the children will be killed."

I sat there a minute, debating whether I should go back and join the children so I could die with them (I was absolutely serious) or whether I should stick around where I was so that I could tell Conn to curse God and die when the tree fell. Then all of a sudden it was as if someone had turned on a light in my mind. I realized who Job's enemy really was! It wasn't God at all—and neither was ours. Satan had been *allowed* to test Job! Was it possible that I had finally stumbled onto the answer to our own miseries? I knew with a rush of relief that I was right. With tears of release streaming down my face I ran to the bathroom—the only place in the trailer where I could be alone. For the first time in ten days I began to praise God for being my God and for so carefully, tenderly taking care of us through it all. My turning point had finally come.

I do not want to give the impression for even an instant that from that moment on all our problems were solved and I became Miss Merry Sunshine for the whole group. The problems were a long way from solved and I would still have moments of doubt, depression, and anger, but from that time on as we chose to believe God and His Word—all of it, but especially Romans 8:28—we were given the priceless gift of hope. We did not have instantaneous peace of mind nor did we have a constant bouyant joy; but we did enjoy the cherished, irreplaceable satisfaction that we were indeed a part of God's family and that He was definitely acting on our behalf. Nothing had really changed on the outside, but in recognizing the enemy we had become a part of the solution.

The mud still had to be dug out of the house; it was an unbelievably awful mess. But gradually our sense of humor, which had completely disappeared with the furniture and the barn, began to return. As I shoveled out the kitchen one day, throwing the mud grandly out of the place where there used to be an east window, I looked toward the east end of the farm and saw a lovely waterfall. It was not exactly Niagara, but the tremendous force of the river had cut a huge hole in the land, and under other circumstances and in other places it would have been quite a pretty sight.

"Look, honey," I said to Conn as he walked through the kitchen. "We've got our own private waterfall in the east forty. Want to go on a honeymoon?" It was a pretty feeble attempt at a joke, but he was with me all the way.

With an evil glint in his eye, as if he had waited twenty-five years for the opportunity, he answered instantly, "No, thanks, Clare, I've got a real headache!"

For the first week or two, the task before us seemed so monstrous that it was not only hard to know where to begin, but anything that was done seemed insignificant in the light of everything that was left undone. Debris was piled to a depth of thirty feet or more around the trees that remained in the yard. Dead animals caught there began to decay. With giant bulldozers, friends who had come to help hacked away at the heap, only to create another problem: where to deposit the resulting tons of trash. It was like that time after time: one problem solved seemed to create two others. But gradually, order began to develop out of chaos, both physically and spiritually.

The girls and their husbands had come to help, along with several other friends from California, and just in their coming they had been a tremendous morale booster for all of us. But each member of the family found he was facing the same nemesis—a colossal feeling of inadequacy and guilt that he was not able to accomplish more.

I know now that that was a result of two things. First, the task itself was so formidable that everyone had to work independently of the other. One of the lessons we learned from that was how terribly important it was for everyone to actually get together every morning, touch base, and pray and ask God to direct us as a unit. I know everyone was praying individually, but we needed to pray together. In the urgency of getting the job done as soon as we possibly could, and because we were all staying at different places in the valley, we didn't do that. I would never want to repeat that mistake. It was far too costly! I know that both Conn and I were aware of the need, but in the stress of the moment and the shock of the loss, we didn't do it.

Neither of us were aware, at that point in our lives, how much every Christian is in need of authority and direction from God through human channels—men God has chosen to interact in our lives. As a woman, I had

121

known for years the comfort and security of having a godly man as my leader, friend, comforter and protector. I was not committed to Conn as my *authority,* but I was committed to him as my *husband.* According to God's own Word, that put me in the position of following Conn as he was led by God.

Many times since we became Christians, Conn made decisions I did not agree with one hundred percent, or sometimes much less than that. But as we prayed together and shared completely and openly all the facts and feelings we had about that particular subject, God gave us both the freedom to say what we thought and then, in trust, to ask Him to give Conn the right path to follow. He has never failed to provide Conn with the leadership he has needed, and He also has never chosen to lead this family through me!

But I know my freedom to share with Conn completely and without reservation any input I have has been an enormous help to both of us. There have been many times when my objections or endorsements have definitely weighed heavily in his decisions, but I have the tremendous freedom of knowing that Conn does not have to build his case on my feelings or facts. That gives me enormous security; I do not have to bear the weight of decisions that are not mine to make. At the same time, I know God uses me in my ordained place as a wife to shape Conn's judgment and direction. In every way Conn has become my covering of love.

I do not ask Conn what to do in every situation I am faced with on a daily basis. After all, God has given me intelligence and experiences that not only allow me to cope with life, but sometimes give me more expertise than Conn. He would be very upset if I suddenly began to ask his advice and counsel in every area of homemaking, writing, and speaking; it would not only be superfluous, but it would actually insult his intelligence as well as mine.

Besides, I know Conn and I know what he wants and expects in our home and our family. I don't have to ask him to correct Jon or one of the girls if they misbehave when I am home and he is not. He doesn't want our children to be rude or disrespectful, so he has a right to expect me to guide and correct them when necessary. We have lived together and shared together and prayed together long enough that I know his desires as well as I know my own, and there is no need to consult him at every turn. But there are many times of confusion or questioning or illness or stress, when I definitely don't just *want* his covering; I *must* have it or I simply cannot function!

After the flood, in those times of confusion and difficulty, Conn and I both realized I was not the only one who really needed authority and covering; Conn needed it too. We were simply not aware, until the conference in Ohio, that Conn could have that God-appointed oversight and direction from the church itself.

We had known many pastors in our lives, men we had greatly loved and respected. But they were not our authority because we had never committed ourselves to them in that capacity, nor had they committed themselves to us in that way. They were marvelous friends, and many times Conn had shared with them, but we had a much greater need than for simple friendship.

We needed men who were committed to God and to us as a loving, serving authority—men to whom we gave the freedom to direct our lives as God led them. You do not do that lightly; it took many months of soul-searching and praying and asking God's guidance before we dared commit ourselves to our by-now newly formed church group and ask them to be our apostles and elders.

This made a big difference in our lives and the way we were finally able to handle the crises at that time. If we were to face another crisis, we would have the assurance of men who would not only come but would have the authority to tell us to do what they believed was the right thing. We would have the freedom of not only having people with whom to share the burden but also of knowing they were completely committed to seeing God's will in our lives and were quite willing to do whatever was necessary to see that that will was carried out. Believe me, it makes all the difference in your security or lack of it!

During that time I saw not just the strengths and weaknesses of the church as such, but I also saw—in living color, and almost as painfully—the strengths and weaknesses of my own family. It was really agonizing at times, but it was also a tremendous growing experience for all of us, with a lot of beauty in it to soften the hard places. Our family is stronger and more loving and compassionate than they were before, but I don't want anyone to have the slightest doubt that if Christ had not been the center of each of our lives, we would not only have come out of it blemished, we would have been shattered.

Jesus Christ holds this universe together; He is also the bond for a family and a home. He gave us the grace to see each other's imperfections and to continue to love, not in spite of them, but because of them! He gave each of us the freedom to be completely wrong and angry and guilty, and still be completely and freely loved by everyone else. Who in the world but God could possibly do that? Each of the childrens' reactions to news of the dam failure and the events of the following days were very revealing to this mother, as I saw how individually and specially God was molding each of my children as they were maturing in Christ.

On the day of the dam collapse itself, Lisa heard the

news as it was flashed as a news bulletin on television throughout the nation. Almost at the same moment, Carl called from Rexburg to tell her that he and Julie were all right, but that they had no news of the rest of us.

"Lisa," he began his conversation, "the Teton Dam has broken and we all have had to evacuate."

"What about Mom and Dad and the kids?" Her voice did not sound like her own. She could not believe what she was hearing!

"I don't know. Mom called about noon and said the dam was having trouble, but I don't have the slightest idea where she and the kids are. Dad is at a conference."

"What can I do to help?" The words came automatically to Lisa's lips. She felt our loss as if it were her own, and indeed, in many ways I suppose it really was.

The hours dragged on. The news bulletins were increasingly discouraging as more was known, including the climbing death toll. Dave, Lisa's young husband, came home as soon as he heard what had happened. Putting his strong arms around her, they cried together as they watched the latest news release showing the water covering the valley they had both come to love. In vain they watched for some familiar landmark. There was nothing. Hesitatingly, not really wanting to know, and yet compelled to ask, Lisa finally turned to Dave and put into words the question she had been thinking all afternoon. "Can the house stand the pressure of all that water, Dave? Just in case they didn't get out in time, I mean?"

She knew Dave would answer honestly, and that he should. He is a young building contractor who had worked for Conn for several years. That was when he and Lisa had met. After seven years of waiting, in October of 1974 they were married in St. Anthony in the same small church where Conn and I had been married twenty-five years before.

Dave knew the house well, and he had also seen the dam. He had studied the construction of the old house, which fascinated him. Dave is one of those remarkable people who is vitally interested in *everything,* and he will be forever welcome in any group because of his vibrant, exuberant personality. He knew the house had been very well built, with a design that would help it withstand a great deal of stress. But he also knew, as a builder, that it could have some very real limitations in the flood because of its old foundation. Throughout the afternoon he had been silently praying that that part of the house could stand up to what would amount to unbelievable stress from the billions of gallons of water that must have been in the Teton Dam.

"I just don't see how it can, Lisa," he replied as gently as he could to Lisa's question. "But I do feel very sure your folks got out all right."

The phone began to ring as friends got word of the dam break and realized how close we were to it. To each of them Dave gave the same message: "All we know is what we have seen on TV. We do know that Julie and Carl and the girls are safe in Rexburg. They got out in plenty of time. We'll call you back as soon as we hear anything else."

Dave tried in vain to call Larry and Beck in Texas. For hours there was no answer. Together they waited and prayed for the safety of all of us.

At last, exhausted with the waiting and tension and giving up hope that they would hear anything else that night, Dave and Lisa tucked their tiny son Charlie into his crib and decided to call it a day. They turned out the lights for a night of sleep they knew would probably never come, just as the phone rang again—for the hundredth time, it seemed. Wearily, ready to tell another friend that they still knew nothing at all, Lisa picked up the phone and heard the beautiful sound of Beck's voice.

"Are you okay, honey?" The typical older sister, Beck wanted to make sure Lisa was holding up. Together they cried and consoled each other. Beck and Larry had just heard of the disaster.

Realizing that neither of them knew of anything other than Julie and Carl's safety, they promised to call each other as soon as they heard any news or could get a call through to St. Anthony. Since all the phone lines were down in the area, it was nearly impossible to get any information.

There was very little I could tell Beck when I finally got through to her the next day. "How soon can we come, Mom?" There was no question in any of our minds whether or not they *would* come—the only question now was timing. I was grateful for that. I wanted them with me, for their sake as much as for mine. Almost any situation is bearable if you know exactly what you are facing, and to be a long way away and feel completely helpless is very difficult.

"I'll call Lisa and Dave for you. I know they are planning to come. How soon do you want them, and is there anything either of us can bring along?"

Conn took the phone and told Beck to tell our friends who wanted to help that we had two tremendous needs at the moment: manpower to help dig out and money to begin rebuilding. We knew we would have to get a loan for the formidable job of rebuilding, but we had no idea how long it would take or indeed, whether anyone would even lend money on a farm that might or might not ever be farmable again!

We hung up, our load much lighter now that it was shared with those we loved, and began our busy day. In the meantime, Beck had called Lisa and both couples began to make plans for the trip to Idaho. Larry had to get an emergency leave from the Air Force; Dave had to arrange to leave his business at the height of the season.

127

But without the slightest hesitation or concern for their own welfare, the two couples were on their way to us within hours.

On that Christmas Eve long ago, when I had shared with Conn my deepest desires, I had no idea that it would take a flood to show me how completely and abundantly God had answered my three wishes. I knew Lisa and Dave loved Beck and Larry with deep affection. Both couples were hurting so for Julie and Carl, as well as for Nancy and Jon and us. I knew if it were possible they would have traded places with us without a moment's hesitation. "How rich I am, after all!" I thought, as I hung up the phone. God not only gave me that second wish, He had let me *see* it answered beyond anything I could ask for! Double blessing!

The second wish was answered, and so was the first. In the frightening days immediately after the flood I began to see Conn with new eyes, and I realized that God had answered my desire for a deep and growing marriage relationship in a way I could never have imagined. In all the years Conn was in business in California, I had never really seen him in action as he dealt with the thousands of problems inherent in any enterprise. But now, as I watched him I was staggered by the problems that faced us and by his remarkable reaction to them, especially after the first few days of shock wore off.

Within three days after the flood, Conn's first constructive thought was that we had to be back together again as a family. He had stayed out at the farm at night since the first Sunday after the collapse, because of the enormous looting that started almost immediately.

Nancy and Jon and I stayed at a friend's home in town. While the offer of Don and Marie Douglass's home was one of the kindest things that happened to us all week, we all realized very quickly how much we needed to be together. The government had promised to move mobile homes into the area for temporary housing, but both Conn and I had some misgivings about how long it would take to get the program in motion and what they would be like once they arrived. So Conn went to a local dealer and bought a three-bedroom trailer to move to the farm so that we could be a family physically again.

Although it took weeks for the river to return to its original bed, by the third day it had greatly receded. Pole Line Road, however, which borders one side of our farm, was still almost nonexistent at that point. Using every kind of heavy equipment available and dozens of men, the Army Corps of Engineers began working on it within twenty-four hours after the flood. The road is the shortest way to the areas of the valley affected by the dam break.

Very early on the third day, as the engineers prepared to continue filling gaping holes in the road and building temporary bridges, out of St. Anthony came this lumbering monster of a truck pulling a seventy-foot trailer. It went through the first roadblock without a hitch—the guards' mouths simply hung open. After all, they were there to prevent people from looting and taking things *out,* and the last thing they expected to see was something like that going *in!*

The truck crept along the road, straining but crossing the temporary bridges—while everyone collectively held their breath. At last, late in the morning, the truck came to within fifty feet of the lane leading to the farm. There the driver, my husband, encountered the first real trouble. The temporary road, which was not nearly completed, was only ten feet wide; the wheels on the trailer were twelve feet wide. But Conn moved ahead, realizing too late the road was too narrow. Conn said later it was the first time in his life, and he sincerely hoped it was the last, that he nearly lost two houses within seventy-two hours!

Everything ground to a halt. The trailer made the road not only impassable but also completely unavailable for further construction. The Army refused to widen the road with the trailer sitting on it; Conn refused to have the trailer taken back to town when it was so close to the farm. The county commissioners were called.

At first they tried to be sweetly reasonable.

"Please, Mr. Bauer, you can see the trailer is blocking the road. It must be moved."

Conn couldn't have agreed more; he had never intended to set up housekeeping in the middle of the road. He would be very happy to have some help to move it on its way.

Now the commissioners were starting to steam. "Either move it or we will have it bulldozed out of the way!"

Conn was unimpressed. Photographers from the local paper were already there to take pictures of the first mobile home to go into the stricken area. How would it look for the county to wreck a person's replacement home when the government dam had ruined his first one? It was, after all, an election year.

Patiently, Conn explained once more that the sooner he got some help to move the mobile home onto the farm, the sooner they could get on with their work on the road. But that was apparently too easy. The commissioners called the head of the engineer corps.

Conn greeted the head of the corps pleasantly when he came out from town, and said if they were willing to work together they could have the trailer off the road and on its way toward the farm in a very few minutes. The commander saw little to be pleasant about. "Get that trailer moved!" was his express command.

"Fine," said Conn. "Widen the road and we'll be on our way."

Stubborn farmer! The state governor was called. I have always wondered if they had a backup call to the White House prepared, just in case. Cecil Andrus (now Secretary of the Interior) is not your run-of-the-mill politician. This man of rare common sense, whose care and concern for each of us affected by the flood made all of us forever grateful to him, gave one quick order: Help move the trailer onto the farm, finish the road as soon as possible, and do it now! By late afternoon the trailer was safely settled at the farm.

From that moment on Conn rarely saw a problem. He had some bad days, depressed at times by the enormity of the problems we were facing. At times he felt none of the rest of us were any help at all; we all had moments like that. But more and more he began to see the problems as challenges for which God would provide an answer.

Joyce Landorf visited us several months after the flood, and she asked Conn if any one thing had helped in that time more than anything else. Conn said yes, that Romans 8:28 had made a big difference.

That response was a little surprising for Joyce. Several years earlier when her husband, Dick, had been kidnapped and then finally returned home, they had repeated Romans 8:28 all night long. But it did not give them the peace and comfort they hoped it would, Joyce said.

"Oh, it didn't give me any *peace,*" replied Conn "What it gave me was hope!" There is a tremendous difference between peace and hope, and what we needed for those first few weeks was a living hope. God gave us that.

Some time after the waters had completely receded from the farm, Conn asked me if I would like to take a walk with him out into the fields to see the extent of the

damage. I didn't really want to go at all, but I knew
sooner or later I had to see it. More than that, I knew
Conn wanted some company while he walked.

We kept carefully to the higher ground wherever we
could because much of the ground was still soggy from
the flood and the rains that had followed. Gradually I
realized we were approaching our erstwhile waterfall.
There in the field—where once had been a peaceful
pasture—was a giant hole, nearly as big as a football field
and ten to twelve feet deep! The land had been torn away
far below the bedrock with a force it was impossible for
me to comprehend. I looked at the hole and saw only a
place where we would never again grow crops.

"What on earth are we going to do with this? Just give
it up for dead loss and hope no one falls into it?" My mind
searched for a possible use for the hole and came up with
nothing.

"It's not nearly the problem it looks like, honey,"
Conn's answer came quickly and firmly. "You see, the
flood left deposits of sand and gravel from the dam all
over the farm, and all we really have to do is start spreading some of it in this direction. Actually, this old hole is
going to be a big help. Without it we'd have had a long
haul to get rid of the debris and stuff that got dumped
onto the place."

That was his approach to everything that was happening around us. I had known for years there was no way
Conn could have been the success in business he had
been without a very special wisdom and strength and
balance, but the flood gave me the chance to see this
magnificent man in action. I will be grateful to God for
that all my life.

Yes, God had answered that long-ago first Christmas
wish with His usual class and abundance. The dream for
a growing, loving marriage was truly fulfilled.

132

9

God at Work Through His Own

One of the interesting things about watching several children grow up is learning that they each have very different strengths and weaknesses, temperaments and dispositions. I have always known that one of my children was adopted, but I have often forgotten which one it is!

When Christ came into each one of our lives, nobody's personality really changed. We became much more balanced and enjoyable and easier to live with, but a lot of the old personality was completely recognizable. I understood that perfectly. God still has a lot of work to do in my life, too.

In a crisis, both the best and the worst of any person's nature comes out. As I watched each of the girls and Jon react to the flood from a basic level, I was both greatly encouraged at what God had done and a little overwhelmed at how much there was still left to do.

Julie, our oldest daughter, is by birth and by temperament the leader of the children. Throughout childhood she was enormously responsible and careful. She was also the most outspoken and honest of the children. I could depend on her to watch over the younger children, and she ruled them with an iron hand even when she was not in charge. She is very tender and loving, with a delightful sense of humor and an explosive temper, and through the years we all learned to avoid setting it off at all costs.

Julie asked Christ into her life because she was intrigued by the changes He was making in me. My temper was as fierce as hers and as she watched Him begin to make me more stable and less inclined to displays of temper, she wanted to know Him, too. She was slow and far less impulsive about asking Christ to be her Lord and Savior than either Beck or Lisa. She had been the leader for a long time, and for months she weighed the cost of inviting Him to take that place before she dared go through with the invitation. But once Julie made the commitment she did it as she had done everything else in her life—without reservation. She gave her life totally to Jesus, and gradually He began to change her. It was both fascinating and heartbreaking to watch her struggle at times.

She did not become less of a leader. On the contrary, that quality was enhanced in her life. There was a direction and a purpose and a challenge in her life that gave her leadership a new dimension. Within months after her commitment to Christ she had become an A student, and for the last two years of high school and during college she never missed being on the dean's list. The ruling passion of her life was horseback riding. She was determined to ride on the U. S. team in the Olympics.

Conn held a riding clinic at the stable, conducted by the equestrian coach of the Olympics, in order to assess Julie's chances for making the team. His verdict was curt. The girl was very good, but her horse would never last through the Pan-Am games, let alone the more grueling Olympic events. Since there was no time to train another horse, she did not stand a chance of going to the top. It was a difficult time for all of us, but the dream was finally put to rest.

From that time on, the focus of Julie's life changed from equestrian events to her college career and a young man named Carl Blanton, who was becoming more and more familiar to our family. In December of 1970, Julie and Carl were married in a beautiful Christmas wedding.

Their marriage was not quite as beautiful as the wedding, for a few years at least. There were a thousand adjustments for both of them to make, as there are in any marriage. These adjustments were compounded by the fact that they decided, after much prayer and counseling, to go on staff with Campus Crusade for Christ. Carl's dedication and love for God equaled Julie's, and together they wanted to serve Him with all their hearts.

Unfortunately, Carl is the youngest child in his family by several years. To combine Julie's assertiveness and his passivity created some very real problems for their marriage. These problems were solved with some difficulty during the early years of their marriage. But when lively little Rebecca appeared on the scene, times became much tougher for them.

For several reasons they decided to leave Campus Crusade and move to Idaho not long after we had come. Work was difficult to find, and when Carl eventually got a job it didn't offer him time or opportunity to express his creativity, as photography had done. Only the fact that they could take their problems and questions and frustrations to God made those days bearable at all—not a bit easy, but bearable. Amanda Clare joined their home in December of 1975. Her personality was much like Carl's—gentle, undemanding, and loving—whereas Rebecca had always been much more outgoing, demanding, and *definite*.

Late in May of 1976, just a few weeks before the flood struck, Julie was hospitalized for several weeks for a severe and nearly incapacitating back injury. Carl's beautiful mother Mildred came from San Jose and cared for the girls and Carl while Julie was undergoing treatment in the hospital. Mildred left for home Saturday morning, June 5, the day after Julie came home from the hospital. Julie was still suffering the excruciating headache that so often follows the X-rays and drugs inherent in back treatment, but she was delighted to be home again with Carl and the girls. Carl took his mother to the airport that morning and had not been home long when they received word they must evacuate because of the flood.

In the days following the flood, both of them were in deep shock. Carl's pictures and slides that had been such a vital part of his work and, to a very large degree, one of his deepest satisfactions in life, were completely swept away. He spent futile hours searching the fields looking for them. Most of the slides were never found.

Meanwhile, Julie's temper began to flare more often as she dealt with severe pain, demanding children, the need for housing in an area that suddenly had none at all, and now Carl's seemingly endless, fruitless search.

Psychologists tell us there are three reasons why we become angry—frustration, pain, and fear. (The Bible certainly indicates there is such a thing as righteous anger, but perhaps we hear so little about it because it is so rare.)

Julie was experiencing, to the highest degree, all three of the causes at the same time. She was almost totally frustrated as she watched Carl search for something she felt certain was probably ruined beyond hope or lost forever. She had learned as a young child that things are not always fair in life, and that there are some times when you simply have to admit defeat and go on. She couldn't understand why Carl couldn't see that. But Carl, a youngest child and virtually an only one, had not learned that lesson nearly so well, and for days he hung on to his fruitless search. The longer he looked the more frustrated Julie became.

She was also filled with pain and fear, both mentally and physically, as she looked to Conn and me for help and found there was none to be had. We were as distraught as she was, and she had never seen us that way. Conn had always been able to handle anything, and now his heartbreak and grief made her afraid. I was so tired and confused and angry in those first days that I too could not reach out to Julie. She saw her whole world crumbling around her and there was nothing she could do about it. She was paralyzed with grief and guilt.

In addition to her emotional pain she was still in much physical pain from her back problem, and without realizing it she began to take more and more of the codeine and other drugs that had been prescribed for her. Over and over the prescriptions were renewed by simple phone calls to doctors who agreed without realizing how much was actually being used. The drugs were largely depressants, and instead of helping they only compounded the problem. It was rapidly approaching a serious degree when Beck came from Texas and realized from her years of working in a pediatrician's office that Julie had a definite drug problem. Beck told her bluntly to throw the things out.

Beck's coming was like a breath of fresh air. As she talked to Julie and told her what she saw, Julie realized that somebody was finally offering help and she gratefully took Beck's advice. There were some withdrawal symptoms, but because Beck was there to pray with Julie and help with the girls so Julie could rest and sleep soundly, the situation began to slowly come around.

Because Beck had helped Julie to start talking out her problems, her anger faded and finally she and Carl were able to start communicating again. They talked for hours, and together they prayed. Carl cried one long night as he realized his slides and pictures were gone and he would not find them, but the next morning he was ready to accept the loss and begin again.

As the summer progressed, God gave Carl a new freedom to be the leader in their home in a brand new way, and Julie responded to that leadership with joy and love. Today their marriage is better than it ever has been. Carl is still gentle and creative, but having survived the flood, he and Julie know they can come through any trial because of their dependence on God and His faithfulness.

As a second child, Beck has always been content to be number two. It didn't bother her to follow Julie—she enjoyed it! Beck has never had a problem with a temper; moodiness proved a much better weapon for her. She has a very real stubbornness that does not come through as a bad character trait. In fact, she has always been so nice about it that it comes through as a virtue most of the time. When Beck starts a job she will finish it if it kills her—and if you are the one who must wait for her to get it done, it might kill you too in the process. But by and large Beck was an easy child to raise, care for, and live with.

Early in life she developed a very real gift of seeing needs and wanting to do something about them. Years ago, while I was still managing the stable in Monte Sereno, I often came home late in the evening almost too tired to stand up. Many of those times, Beck, who was still a teen-ager, would gently take my hand and say, "Mom, I'm really in a mood to cook tonight. Would you mind if I take over? I'd really like to!"

There isn't much doubt in my mind that on many of those occasions fixing dinner was the last thing Beck had in mind ten minutes before, but she simply anticipated the need and acted on it. I felt she saved my life several times!

The one thing Beck could not bear is open confrontation. She is very sensitive to others, and to confront or challenge others was not simply difficult for Beck; it was almost impossible. She would rather do almost anything than be caught in the middle of a battle—or worse, be the cause of one. I appreciated that facet of her personality, but it caused me a lot of concern when she was a teenager. I knew it would be very easy for her to go along with the crowd and do things she knew were wrong, simply because she didn't want to hurt anyone's feelings.

In the past few years she has learned to say no much more effectively—extremely well, I might add, since the birth of Jonathan Lee, the first child to come into her and Larry's home. But it will probably forever make Beck slightly ill to face a battle between two people she loves and cares for. She is a born peacemaker, and she found that the flood zone, and particularly our home at times after the flood, was a battleground time and again.

Larry is as much a part of our family as Beck. I fell in love with him the first day I met him, and although Beck was dating several other young men at the time, I told the Lord that if it was all right with Him I thought Larry was exactly right to be Beck's husband. An oldest son, he provided the leadership Beck needed, and with compassion and joy he fills in the places Beck lacks. His love for Beck is exceeded only by his love for God.

His parents are some of our dearest friends, and I will be forever grateful to God that Larry, like David and Carl, is a part of our family. Larry makes us laugh. He knows when humor is needed, and just as important, he is gifted in knowing when it is *not*. They are a very special couple, and within days after the flood, they came.

It was to be a very difficult time for both of them. In so many of the situations that faced us there was simply nothing anyone could say or do—and how they both wanted to help. But with a wisdom born of God that was far beyond their years or experiences, they responded as listeners, as mud shovelers, and as a touching, caring family. Their presence helped make us whole again.

There were many confrontations for Beck as she got caught in the angry frustration of each of us at one time or another, and it was a very growing time for her. She learned that you do survive them. She went through a time of feeling constantly guilty that she could not do more and be in several places at the same time. When I face a crisis of grief or death today, I know from watching Beck and Larry that it is not necessary to have a lot of pat Christian answers; it is only necessary to love and hold and comfort. They did that for us.

Lisa is our middle child. So many times in the years she was growing up she *felt* like a middle child. She developed a shyness and reserve that does not always show to outsiders. Along with that shyness, she also seemed to develop a tremendous sensitivity to everyone around her, especially to those who are hurting or frightened or alone. Lisa did not hesitate a moment to reach out to us when she heard of the flood. She and I have shared a special closeness for years, and she hurt so terribly for me.

First, she asked what she could do to help. Then, in a way that was anything but typical for Lisa, she went after that help. It has always been unbearably difficult for her to talk to others, especially to people she does not know. Now she was not only going to talk to them, she was going to ask them for help! Her motto became, "All I have to lose is my pride," and away she went. She was determined that our lives and the farm and home would be salvaged and restored if she had to do the job singlehandedly! She told me later that often she had to sit in her car for ten minutes or longer, praying for the strength and courage to ask, but as she asked, God gave her what she needed.

One of the places Lisa believed she should go for help was to the Christian school in San Jose where she and our other children had been students. Conn had served on their board for years and had been one of the school's biggest boosters. Without much hesitation, but with more than a little prayer and trembling, Lisa marched into the office of the school's principal, explained the situation, and asked for help.

When I heard later about Lisa doing that, I was torn between laughing and crying. It isn't what a person can afford to give that really constitutes the gift—it's what it costs to give it. And I will forever suspect that Lisa's reaching out in love to help us must rate as one of the more expensive gifts ever given.

She and Dave came. Along with little Charlie, our very special grandson, they came—in their pickup loaded down with mud pumps, blankets, towels, and all Lisa's lovely things that she wanted me to have to make up for losing mine! Dave's help was invaluable to Conn, as he worked the mud pumps and other equipment to try to clear the mud from the basement and the rest of the place. Lisa's gift was that of comfort and cooking and just being there. I held Charlie and loved him, and as he laughed and cooed and we enjoyed one another, my world regained some of its lost perspective. God was still at work in our lives.

At fifteen, Nancy's world had come crashing apart, and both she and Jon felt terribly helpless to put it back together again. She is a gentle person. For years she could be found in her bedroom curled up with a book, perfectly content to let the rest of the world go by. Gradually, after the move to St. Anthony, she began to change and become much more outgoing. She developed a good sense of humor, and in the years preceding the flood after the older girls were gone from home, Nancy and I became very close. She took piano, ballet, and tap-dancing lessons, and it seemed at times that we lived in the car driving to and from one studio or another. But the lessons gradually paid off. Over the years, as Nancy's expertise at the piano began to increase by leaps and bounds, she would sit down at the piano, when she sensed I was sad or lonely, and play the beautiful Brahms or Chopin or Beethovan that never failed to lift me and help get my world back in focus. It was her love gift to me, and in giving it she received joy as well.

Nancy could not bring herself to go out to the farm for days after the flood. She could not bear to see the general destruction, but especially that of her music and her piano. I told her we would replace the piano as soon as we could, but it was rather like losing a pet—you still have to get over the loss.

Within a few weeks we did get a small spinet piano to keep in the trailer so Nancy could start playing for all of us again. The first day it came she sat for hours and played from memory all the songs she could remember. Tears streamed down her face as she played, but she was not sad. She was starting to get her world back, and she was beginning to see that it would not always be confused and muddy and difficult and lonely.

Nancy committed her life to God when she was only five, and I have never doubted either her commitment or her sincerity. In those days after the flood, she vividly understood in a new way that things do not always go the way we want them to go, but that in spite of that God is still in control, and He does hear and answer our prayers.

Jon went through the same anger and grief all of us experienced, with the additional fright of his near-accident on the tractor. Months after the flood I asked him why on earth he had come back to the farm when he was safely out. He told me he *had* to come back. "You hadn't followed me out like you said you would, and I thought if you had to die there I didn't want you to be alone." I repeat: It is an awesome thing to watch a boy become a man.

Jon worked with Conn, mainly by finding things that had been buried in the mud and working to restore them. For some reason their collection of rifles and pistols and shotguns, of which they were both very proud, did not wash away with everything else. They were found buried deep in the mud, and for hours on end Jon painstakingly took them apart and washed and oiled them. Often tears of rage at the condition of his beloved collection blinded his eyes so that he could hardly see what he was doing. Once in a while the frustration would become too great and he would throw down whatever he was doing, jump on his dirt bike, and race off through the fields, trying to escape from this nightmare.

Those trips rarely failed to anger and provoke Conn, who saw Jon as trying to steal away from the work that Conn considered so overwhelming that every hand was constantly needed. He said later that he realized at the time how irrational his rage was, but he was unable to keep it from surfacing at times.

In those weeks following the flood, all of us had moments of anger and bitter frustration. I know they were necessary in God's economy and love, because without the difficult times we could not have experienced His healing touch later on. But we also needed to understand how impossible it is to separate the physical from the spiritual. God had not left us for a moment, but in our extreme weariness and pressure there were many times when we were even too tired to pray. I am forever grateful for a God who understands that, and who not only loves us continually and constantly, but who lets us go through the hard times. Those times of deep crisis become a focal point from which we can minister compassionately to others.

Years before they were even born, I had wanted children who would love each other with a growing love that would become stronger and more beautiful over the years. It took a disaster for me to see how wonderfully God had developed that in our family. I think the imperfections and flaws each one of us displayed only made us appreciate more the grace and power of God. Because God was there, ministering and loving through each of us, we have experienced the very special kind of love that is constructive and gentle and kind and everlasting.

10

The Lessons We Learned

In shady green pastures so rich and so sweet,
God leads His dear children along.
Where the water's cool flow bathes the weary one's feet,
God leads His dear children along.
Some through the waters, some through the flood,
Some through the fire, but all through the blood.
Some through great sorrow, but God gives a song
In the night places and all the day long.

The old hymn says it so very well. The Christian life is not always easy, and certainly never dull. The one thing we can count on is that we are not alone and God will supply whatever we need. There is sometimes a time lag between our knowing that and our experiencing it, and occasionally we are put in what seems to be an endless holding pattern, but God will never fail us. He cannot.

Months after the dam break, a headline in a local paper came leaping out at me. "Designed to Fail?" it read. The long article that followed was a climax of months of investigation by a private firm regarding the collapse of the structure. Their conclusion was that given that particular geographical location, the materials used in the construction, and many other factors involved, the dam failure was inevitable. According to them, it was only a matter of timing.

I do not know how conclusive their study was; the

arguments will probably go on for years. But I do know there are many parallels between the dam and my life.

I, too, was designed with the capacity to fail. The Bible tells us that every person born since Mother Eve was created comes into this world as a sinful human being; thus we are separated from God. Because of our estrangement from Him we are self-centered and continually searching for some kind of satisfying fulfillment that will honestly and completely give our lives meaning and direction. We want a purpose in life that will somehow set us apart as worthwhile persons and give us a reason for living.

With everything in us we try to become what the world calls a success—a powerful person in the field of finance or influence, one who possesses a captivating physical appearance, or one who holds several degrees from a well-known university. While there is certainly nothing wrong with any of those aspirations in themselves— wealth, beauty, and intelligence—they offer no guarantee that we will become the successes we want to be. We may, indeed, have any or all three of those symbols and still find ourselves in despair.

There is still that God-shaped vacuum (so well described by French philosopher Pascal) that can never be filled by anything but the creator God Himself, made known through Jesus Christ. Empires can be built on an earthly plain without thought of God, but no one has yet found lasting satisfaction apart from Him. There is always another mountain to climb, another world to conquer.

The void is filled on that day when we are born for the second time by asking Jesus to come into our lives and make us the persons He wants us to be. In that moment we become new creatures, and from that day on we have the potential for success, the power to accomplish, and the reality of satisfaction of the deepest kind. We are linked up with the greatest force the world has ever seen, and our lives are daily transformed as we allow Him to work through us to accomplish what we never could alone.

When the dam failed, it destroyed with a wild and unchecked vengeance the very land and homes it had been designed to protect. In my own failure for so many years, I too very nearly destroyed the ones I loved the most, the ones God had given to me to care for and protect. They were the last people on earth I wanted to hurt, yet they were the only ones who fully bore the brunt of my anger and frustration and hostility. However, when Christ came into my life, the changes He made, in some instances at least, were pretty dramatic.

When the dam collapsed, Jon and I nearly drowned for the simple reason that I was looking in the wrong direction for possible danger. I reasoned that the water would have to come from the south when in fact it was coming at us from the opposite direction.

I had made that same mistake years before in not seeing the mortal danger I was in. I had been looking in the wrong direction for solutions to my seemingly unsolvable problems. I looked inside myself, I looked to my husband, my children, and to others around me for happiness and fulfillment, when all the time they were not meant to meet my deepest need. The help I so desperately needed could only come from God, and that could only happen when I admitted I was a sinner in need of a Savior.

I know now that I must have heard the gospel many times in those years of searching, but because I had always equated sin with gross immoral acts such as adultery and murder, I failed to see that I too was a sinner. Of course, I knew I wasn't perfect; I was terribly aware of my shortcomings and failings. But I honestly thought they were simply part of being human, something everyone has to one degree or another. I worried; I was angry; I was guilty; I was moody and critical; but I honestly was unaware that that was sin and that God could actually change it if I would allow Him to.

On the day I finally was forced to look in the right direction, on that blessed day that I finally knew I was very definitely a sinner in need of a Savior who could and would change my life, I was saved from both the power of sin and from myself. But I had to see the danger for what it was before I could see the answer God had for me.

An older couple lived about a mile northeast of us, also near the river. Theirs was one of the prettiest places in the area, with a beautifully kept yard blooming with flowers and shaded by trees all summer long. It looked like a house that was loved and cared for, and I thoroughly enjoyed it every time we drove past. The couple had lived there for many years—all their married life, in fact—and the place had been a secure haven not just for them, but for the family they had raised there as well. Now their children were married and away from home.

On the morning of the dam collapse, a son who lived nearby went to his parents' home to warn them of the coming danger. They appreciated his concern, but said they would stay at the place and care for the animals. The house had seen them through many blistering Idaho summers and through the blizzards and cold of winter, and they saw no reason why it would fail them at this point. So they thanked their son but encouraged him to go on his way. They said they would watch the river and if it began to rise too quickly they would go on their way.

I can understand their actions perfectly, but like me, they were apparently looking in the wrong direction. As they sat in the house talking together, they must suddenly have heard the roar that drowned out all conversation and, rushing to the north windows, saw the unbelievable sight of the horrendous danger *coming from the "wrong" direction!* They ran for their lives to their pickup truck to try to outrun the water. They died in their vehicle, which was still in the yard; the keys were turned on in the ignition, but they were too late. It made me sick when I heard of their tragedy, and it could so easily have been us.

Looking in the wrong direction. How many people today are looking to their little houses made of good works, church membership, Golden Rule keeping, and a thousand other futile gestures for the protection that will fail them when they need it the most?

The question we have been asked the most regarding the dam failure and its impact on our lives is, "What is the most important thing you learned?" I'm never sure there is a pat answer, but I do know our lives will never be the same because of it. Every crisis changes the people involved, for better or for worse. When we face death or irretrievable loss, we are never again the same people we were before. We may become bitter, hostile, angry, and self-pitying. Some people in the area seem to have developed what I call a "flood mentality," a sort of apathetic, who-cares-about-anything-because-it-will-all-probably-get-washed-away-anyway attitude. Or we may see the crisis as a challenge and a gift from God, and therefore something He intends to use to make us more pliable and serviceable for His kingdom from that time on. Our attitudes can change the entire picture. I had some problems in dealing with the time lag I experienced between the actual collapse of our world and the victory that was inevitable as we allowed God to lead us through. In all the things I had read before our tragedy, it seemed people knew immediately (or at least within three days) that everything was going to be just fine. When that did not pan out in my life, I thought there had to be something wrong with either God or me. But there was nothing wrong with either of us; there was simply a necessary time of working through the problems and waiting on God. But the lessons we learned were so valuable that it was worth everything we paid in time and tears and work and wondering.

There was the lesson of Christian fellowship and oneness—the advantages of functioning in a *body* of believers as opposed to traveling alone.

I suppose that in the good times, the easy times of our lives, we can afford to separate ourselves from other Christians and try to have fellowship with God alone. I know the great value of spending time in prayer and meditation and communion with God. Every Christian needs that on a daily basis. But for every believer there is also an untold blessing in watching the body of Christ, His church, functioning as one. And in crisis it is not just a blessing; it is an absolute necessity! Love without arms is not love at all, and as the church gathers around her wounded and weary members to love them and cheer them and help them, everyone in the church—the needy and the helpers—are blessed and strengthened and built up.

When there is honest commitment and love in the church, everyone can dare to be transparent and vulnerable in a way that is truly impossible outside the family of God. And when someone dares to share his fears and failures inside the Christian community, he should not be despised and rejected because of them. We are all built up together as we see and experience the precious fact that our love from God is not on a performance basis, but on a foundation of unlimited, all-encompassing love that sets no boundaries. That has to be one of the most liberating things that can ever happen to any living soul. Someone has said, "God does not love us *because* . . . , He loves us, *period.*" That is incredible! As we allow God to live His life through us, he gives us the freedom to love our fellow Christians in that same way. Without Him there is absolutely no way we can offer uncondi-tional love to others; with Him, it becomes not only possible, but a way of life.

Another lesson that came home with a powerful thrust was that we as Christians have a great ability to hear what God wants us to hear if we are willing to be sensitive and really listen with our hearts as well as our ears. I knew that a long time before the flood, but many times I only heard what I wanted to hear and not what was really being said at all. Either what I was hearing was going to be too upsetting for me to bear or the information would disrupt my tidy world, and so I chose not to really listen at all.

About three weeks before the dam failure I was sitting in church and had a coughing fit. Rather than disrupt the service, I went to the kitchen in the basement for a glass of water. I was standing there when a man came into the room with a look of real agitation on his face. I knew him; he worked at the dam. I walked over to him and said, "What's the matter, Harry? You look like a man with a problem." I hoped he would smile and tell me I was seeing things, that he was not worried about anything in the world. Frankly, I wasn't in the mood to listen to anyone's problems that day.

His answer came, however, without a trace of humor. "I just flew over the dam in a small plane, and I'm worried. You can't believe how fast that reservoir is filling. The water is just coming way too fast!"

He was obviously very worried, but I chose not to pursue the conversation any further. After all, the dam couldn't possibly be full, and what if it was? We couldn't stop the flow of water from the mountains! I left the basement and never mentioned the conversation to Conn.

A very special friend of mine, my sister Betty, has had

cancer. After her first surgery for the disease, as soon as she came out of the anesthetic, she asked the doctor if he had been able to remove all the cancer. His answer to her, as she later recalled, was, "Betty, we did everything we could." Now when you or I hear that we know his answer was certainly not a resounding yes, but that is not what Betty heard. She heard him say what, in that particular moment, she *had* to hear him say. She heard him say, "Yes."

Several weeks later, as she was undergoing chemotherapy, she innocently asked the oncologist why they had to go ahead with this treatment when the cancer had been removed. Astonished, the doctor replied that they had not gotten all the cancer; the chemotherapy was to hold the disease in check until her own immunity would take over. Betty could not believe him, and at his insistence she went back that day to the surgeon, who repeated his exact words—they had done all they possibly could. They had not been able to remove it all.

In relating the story to me months later, Betty said she had heard only what she could bear in that initial conversation, and that God gave her some time to adjust before she was ready to hear the truth.

In the months since the flood I have asked God to let me hear what He is trying to say to me and not what I want to hear to protect myself from being hurt or uncomfortable or miserable. Would my life, or those of my family, have been any different if I had dared to pursue that conversation that Sunday morning? I doubt it, but I will never know. I only know it was a good lesson in listening.

When we returned to the house that first Sunday after the flood, both Conn and I felt a terrible sense of loss that all the things we had loved and furnished our home with for over twenty-five years were gone. Over and over friends told us in the days that followed: things were not important; the important thing was that we were all safe and alive. I knew that was true—of course it had to be. But I had a terrible feeling of guilt because I knew in my heart that the things we had lost were very important to me—all the photo albums and the pictures of the girls and Jon from their babyhood on, our wedding pictures, stitcheries that had been done for me with much love, the book ends Conn and I had bought one day in Mexico after tramping through a small jungle for an hour to reach a tiny village, my autographed books from very special author friends, the Christmas presents the children had made with such care for me as elementary school projects, the collection of crystal apples Conn had started for me in the days when we really couldn't afford them at all, just because he knew I loved them. There is no way to put a value on these things and perhaps we shouldn't, but I did and I still do.

Our lives, you see, do not consist of just this day. They are composites of all our days, and so many of those lost objects were really a part of me that I grieved for that loss terribly. But in the end, God allowed me to see that I could afford to let them go. That lesson was one of the most important I was to learn from the whole experience.

Years before, not long after I had become a Christian, a beautiful and sparkling Christian woman named Joyce Landorf came into my life and our home. God used her to teach me some of the most important things I have come to know.

Joyce does not enter a room; she invades it with her vitality and lively personality! Like Joyce, I had many pretty dishes and silver and napkins and place mats. But unlike Joyce, I did not use these things routinely. I saved them for "special" occasions.

One of Joyce's reigning philosophies is that the nicest people in the world, the most important ones that will ever come into our lives, sit down to eat at our table every night, and they deserve the very best we have—the best china, the best silver, and the best conversation, food, and manners. And so, because of her gentle yet very persuasive influence, I began to use those things. Our mealtimes changed along with nearly everything else in the house in those years after we came to Christ. Dinner quickly became the highlight of the day, and it was there that we not only ate together but also really enjoyed each other's company. Some of our warmest memories were born at that table; and later, as each of the girls married, high on her list of "must haves" were pretty place mats and napkins. They wanted to continue the tradition in their own homes.

That custom was continued in Idaho, and so it was natural that the silver and china and crystal goblets were all in the kitchen. So they went, along with the sink and the dishwasher, when the flood came through. I was sick to find they were gone, but I discovered that one of the real reasons I could finally say good-bye to them was because God had made me aware that they must be *used* and not saved for some mysterious company that would someday be worthy of them. How glad I am that all my children have the memory of being the people for whom I chose the best I had. I would have been filled with regret had I stored those things away to be used for something special, and then had them disappear without being used for the purpose they were designed!

I am more aware than ever that the day will come, probably much sooner than I realize, when God will decide it is time for me or someone I love to come home with Him. Because that is true, I want to be very sure I do not have to regret that I didn't value and cherish and handle and touch each and every relationship in my life. I want my children, my husband, my grandchildren, and my friends to *know* how much I love them and how precious they are to me. I don't want them to have to wait for some special occasion to be told; I want them to be very sure about my feelings today!

It is a habit of my life, as a direct result of experiencing one loss and having the freedom to finally let it go without regrets or guilt, to live each day as if another wave might come rushing in some night and sweep me or the ones who are dear to me right straight into the arms of God. It is not a morbid thought; on the contrary, I think I am more alive than I have ever been because of that realization. Any loss on earth will heal eventually, if it is not compounded or infected with guilt or bitterness. There is probably someone in your life right now who needs to hear that you love him. If you are within reaching distance, someone needs to be hugged. I would do it if I were you; there is always the possibility you will not have the time or the opportunity on another day.

The best lesson, however, and the one I appreciate the most, is the fact that we know beyond a shadow of a doubt that God really is sufficient for all our needs. It is not an academic or theological matter for us any longer. We can be absolutely certain because we have been there, and we know! A Christian is not immune to disaster. If we are going to be triumphant, we are going to have to walk through the mud just like everyone else. But we *are* going to be triumphant in the end, and our pain and suffering will be seen afterward as a time of blessing because we know God was not only in the heartache with us but also actively working on our behalf throughout it all. Maturing in Christ does not come all at once—but after all, growth is what the Christian life is all about.

Epilogue

More than two years have passed since June, 1976. The old log house has been restored and is alive again with the sounds of a family in love with each other and with life itself.

To someone who had never been in this area before the flood, it looks much the same as the rest of southeastern Idaho. It is only when one is made aware that this was the flood's path that all the new houses and young, small trees become acutely noticeable. Only two of the old homes survived the devastation in the area. Very few of the hundreds of huge trees that once sheltered the homes and the lawns were able to withstand the devastating wall of water that came raging from the northeast that lovely summer day. The rare trees that were spared stand like lonely sentinels across the landscape, keeping watch over the fields that are just beginning to be productive again.

Once we had decided, after the tons of mud and debris were laboriously removed from the basement, that the foundation was still intact, we started the massive job of literally rebuilding the old house from the ground up. All the wiring, plumbing, and heating ducts were gone. The plaster had to be removed by hand, down to the lath, and then replaced. The windows were gone; a new sliding door took the place of the huge hole in the south wall of the dining room. The porch that had given me such grief was gone, praise the Lord! Conn says God looked down quietly from heaven that morning of June 5, and said, "Clare, honey, I have good news and bad news. The good news is that I have decided to take care of that porch you have been pestering Me about. The bad news is, I'm going to remove a good portion of the farm with it!" I sincerely doubt that is true, but I do know the veranda that has taken the place of the porch looks for all the world like it has belonged there always! I love it!

It took nearly eight long months to rebuild the house, but in the process of restoration, it became, somehow, more than just the old Bauer house; it became for all the family, and friends as well, a project of love.

Because it was a federal dam that failed, the U. S. government took full responsibility to indemnify those who had suffered losses as a result. To indemnify means simply to restore one to one's former position, as nearly as possible, before the disaster. I would be the first to agree that there is really no way to completely compensate people for the loss of life, property, family treasures, mementos, and pictures, which are forever lost. However, I think it must be said that the people who worked with our claim were more than fair as they endeavored to determine what the losses were and what the replacement value of them actually was. Some things are simply irreplaceable, and there is no way to place a value on them. The only advice I have about that is to enjoy them to the utmost while you can! To put such things as family pictures and heirloom vases in a bank vault would probably insure their safekeeping, but I have always found that the value of any treasure is to be able to see it and hold it and enjoy it. In retrospect, I would still have preferred to enjoy my things and lose them, than to have kept them safe but unreachable!

Julie and Carl are still living in Rexburg; they replaced the home that was swept away with another that is an identical model. Their yard is spectacular in the summer, with hundreds of flowers blooming. Their little girls, Amanda and Rebecca, no longer remember the flood. They seem perfectly secure and show no aftermath from the turmoil of the summer of '76. They are both delightful little girls, mature for their ages. I'm sure part of their security comes from their extended family, which includes Jon, Nancy, Conn, and me. They enjoy coming to the farm and spending the night with us. When they come they cheerfully bid Julie and Carl good night and tell them there is absolutely no hurry about picking them up in the morning!

Lisa and David still live in San Jose with little Charlie, who at the time of this writing is a nice big three-year-old boy. We don't get to see them nearly as much as we would like, and I pray that someday God will see fit to have all my children and grandchildren at least in the same time zone! But until that day comes, we will be content to keep in touch with each other by telephone and letter. Lisa is in a good Bible study in San Jose, and she finds that helps tremendously in keeping her priorities straight, as well as keeping her walk with God consistent and growing.

Beck and Larry are in Texas, although they have been transferred to another air base. Larry was accepted for Officer's Candidate School and is now Lieutenant Larry Cobler. God has blessed them with a little boy, Jonathan Lee. Beck and Larry are in a small but vital Christian fellowship in Del Rio, and I am more than pleased at their growth in Christ. I asked Beck what she attributes that growth to, and without any hesitation she said, "Memorizing Scripture!" Not just verses, mind you, but whole chapters and books! She said she finds that she studies the Word in a different way, as she memorizes the chapter. "It gives me time for it all to really sink in, Mom!" she says quietly. Life has not been particularly easy for Beck and Larry since the flood. For nearly two years, she was unable to become pregnant, and when she finally did, little Jon was born six weeks early. Through it all, she and Larry were able to thank God for the things He was so lovingly teaching them, and now she says she can really minister to others who have to wait for something. And that, my friends, covers a lot of territory!

Nancy is a young woman now, nearly eighteen and a freshman in college. She is deeply sensitive, and of all my children, the most transparent. She tends to be moody and introspective, which can be a real trial to live with, and there have been many times when I have had to remind her that moodiness is a sin. The first time I told her that moodiness is a sin and must be dealt with as such, she was shocked. First my words made her angry, but after she had some time to think about it, she came and said she wanted to apologize. "I just never realized, Mom, that the way I act *does* have an effect on everyone else in the house. I just didn't know that God could do something about my *moods* if I asked Him to!" Her problems didn't all vanish with that one revelation, but like the first step of all long journeys, it was a beginning. Nancy is not just sensitive to her own moods; she is super-sensitive to those of others. Her values have changed in the past three years. Nancy no longer holds things very important in her scale of values. Above all else, she knows that the one possession that can never be taken away is our faith in the Lord Jesus Christ, and she sees others' needs in that light.

I always knew that my life would never be complete without a son, and in Jon, God gave me exactly what I wanted all along! He is now fourteen and becoming more like Conn every day. He is quiet, gentle, and loving. He also loves speed with a purple passion, and enjoys few things more than racing his snowmobile across the fields in the long winter months. His nieces and nephews adore him; Charlie says when he grows up he is going to *be* Jon Bauer! Jon is incredibly patient with all of them, and I

159

love him for it. Little children need a teen-age uncle to look up to! Jon's life is filled with a thousand interests. He is a young man reaching out with strength and excitement for everything life has to offer. When he works, he works with all his heart. When he plays, he does it with enthusiasm.

In the summer of 1978 he went mountain climbing for the first time. He had talked about doing that for years, and when he returned I was anxious to hear about it. It was an unforgettable experience for him, he said, much like a bad case of chicken pox. "Well, I wanted to climb a mountain all my life . . . I'm sure glad *that's* over with!" he told us later. I guess it's always good to know what you don't want to do when you grow up.

Conn and I have found that there are a lot of things in life like that mountain climb! We plan and pray and hope, and then sometimes when we get that for which we planned and prayed, in reality it is nothing like we thought it would be in our daydreams. It is reassuring to know that everything God allows in our lives can not only add a dimension to life but also be something for which we can be profoundly grateful.

A flood was never in our plans or prayers, and yet because of it our lives have been immeasurably enriched. Now we can afford to hold things very loosely, thoroughly enjoying them and delighting in their beauty, but knowing they can be gone in a moment of time. I needed to know that. We see everything we have today as a gift from God and can enjoy it in that light. It is a good way to live.

The meaning of Isaiah 43 has been indelibly impressed upon our minds. "When you pass through deep waters, I will be with you; your troubles will not overwhelm you. When you pass through fire, you will not be burned; the hard trials that come will not hurt you. For I am the LORD your God . . . who saves you" (2,3; TEV).